Commander-in-Failure

By
Kiara Ashanti

No Tomorrow Publishing, LLC

Orlando, FL

ISBN 978-1546730255
Ebook ISBN 1546730257

Cover Design by Steven Novak
http://www.novakillustration.com/- *he's great!*

Edited by Sandra Nguyen
A Fresh Set of Eyes Editing and Writing Services
https://www.facebook.com/SFreshSetofEyes/

Dedication

It may catch you by surprise, but this book is dedicated to the millions of Americans who fought, cried, and voted to put a black man into the White House; proving that widespread racism no longer exists in America.

Contents

FAILURE'S PRELUDE

It is called morbid fascination: the mental state you experience when you rubberneck as you drive by a car wreck. It is the reason some folks flock to house fires or show up at murder scenes. It is how a movie like *Faces of Death* becomes a cult hit and spawns six sequels. It is our inability to look away from something we know is terrible. We must look at it, examine it, process it, and understand it.

It is the exact feeling I had on election night 2008. It permeated my heart, mind, and spirit as I walked into the grocery store and watched people pushing their carts with smiles and hope in their eyes. It is a feeling that clung to me like a lingering depression. For a year, it had been a part of my daily makeup as I watched friends, family, and America caught up in the euphoria of Barack Obama's "Hope and Change" and "Yes We Can" election rallies.

I saw history play out in real time. America was going to elect its first black President. Given that the pain of the sixties and the Civil Rights Movement were only forty years removed, it would be a transformative event. The wounds of the past and America's great moral blight were about to be exorcised.

I should have wept like African-American civil rights leader Rev. Jesse Jackson, who unsuccessfully ran for President in 1984.

I should have been bursting with hope and pride. Pride as an American, and yes, a deeper pride as a black man.

I felt nothing.

I stood transfixed by the historic moment, yes. But what kept me glued to my television as the election results were announced was my morbid fascination at the train wreck about to hit America.

Why did I feel that way? Barack Obama appeared to be the pinnacle of black achievement in America. Columbia and Harvard educated. Married to one wife, with children. A wife who was not white or a fair-skinned model type—yes, the distinction matters for certain segments of the black community. No hidden side chick popped out during the campaign. Obama was not just well-spoken; he was charismatic and thoughtful, too.

He was a perfect prototype of a man who is black who could be President of the United States.

What else could you want? What more could you ask for?

A lot.

A great deal more than Barack Obama had to offer.

This is not and was not a popular view to take as a black person in America. African-Americans are culturally hardwired to pull for the success of other blacks. Modern-day blacks are freer than at any time in history, but for years we were not seen. Most blacks grew up without images of themselves splashed across the covers of magazines. Before the pouty lips of Hollywood megastar Angelina Jolie were called sexy, they were called big and ugly on black women. We did not see ourselves sprinkled on every television show as the likeable or real smart character like gay characters enjoy as a matter, of course, today. *The Cosby Show* was revolutionary not because it showed a life blacks did not have—there were good, loving, black professional families who flowed in money, it's just that we had never seen them on television.

In sports, we dominated the NFL, except in the quarterback position. Until Tiger Woods, golf was a white man's sport as far as blacks were concerned. Tennis was not far behind. I could go on and on, but the point is that when you are not seen or feel like you have not been seen, you root for the person who looks like you when they show up.

As a black person in America, even if you consider yourself conservative, a part of you automatically roots for other blacks. We see Tiger Woods, and without caring about golf, we want him to win. When Venus and Serena Williams hit the court, you root for them and sit down to take in the only tennis match you may watch all year. You want to see two black women succeed in a sport few blacks have played professionally.

We could be talking about sports, a TV show character, a businessman, a politician—it does not matter. If it is a place or position that many blacks don't occupy, you root for them. When an African-American is the first black in anything, we want them to succeed. We take their side. Their success is emotionally our success.

There are many orthodoxies within the black community that I have rejected. There are good reasons for this, and many will be discussed in this book. But I am not immune to this impulse to side with a black person who has broken the color barrier. When Venus and Serena began playing professionally, they became my favorites partly because they were black. That they were excellent and exciting players helped justify my enthusiasm. But if they had not been amazing on the court, I would have still pulled for them. Ditto for Tiger Woods on the golf course. And in college, it felt good to hear people talk about Colin Powell as a possible future President.

So, with all that said, in a world of accomplishments, in a world full of firsts, there is nothing higher than the idea of a black President. Nothing.

N-O-T-H-I-N-G!

When you are by default rooting for the black person in any walk of life, the idea of not rooting for one who is running for US President is blasphemy and inconceivable to many other blacks. Like garbled computer code, it does not calculate.

So, what was wrong with my mental programming?

Why had I endured the stares of family and friends during Obama's two-year campaign for President whenever I said anything negative about him? Why did I put up with being called a traitor, coon, Uncle Tom, brainwashed, and my personal favorite, being told, "You hate yourself? You hate being black?"

I would like to give you an erudite answer steeped in some mind-altering point of view, but I cannot. I could make a case about the philosophical differences between a Democrat and the beliefs I hold dear that make me a conservative, but that is not the reason I never bought into the hype. My reason was a simple requirement I used on all candidates for President.

The presidency is called the *executive* branch because the President is, in effect, the CEO of the country. He cannot dictate decisions like a king. A President has the House and Senate he must work with, just like a Fortune 500 CEO has a board he must work with. The President, however, does set the direction. He is in charge.

Every President *must* have executive experience. They need to have overseen something: a city, a state, a large corporation or nonprofit, a military division. Something where the buck starts and stops with them, because a President's decisions have consequences, simply because they said yes or no. Before they take on the highest office in the land, they must bring to the job a deep understanding of the type of power they are about to wield. That only comes through a prior deep leadership experience.

America's most successful Presidents have all had that in their backgrounds. They have mostly been former governors, but sometimes they were military leaders. Obama was none of these things.

Obama announced his candidacy for President on February 10, 2007, less than two years after becoming a senator for Illinois. By contrast, Hillary Clinton had been a senator for nearly six years. Before becoming a senator, Obama had served as a state-level senator in the Illinois state house, and before that, he was a part-time professor and full-time community organizer.

Race, sex, and political affiliation aside, what in that list of job titles qualifies anyone to be President of the United States? Obama had barely shown up in the Senate before telling the world he was ready to be President.

Obama was not qualified for the job.

I do not say that as political hyperbole. It has nothing to do with the ridiculous idea that he was born in Kenya. He was not, and it would not make a difference if he had been. His mother is American, and therefore he is American. End of discussion.

I am talking about his resume. He had not been a senator for even TWO YEARS before announcing his intention to run for the highest office in the land. This is like getting a job as a retail clerk at Walmart, getting promoted to store manager, and then a year and a half later telling the investors who hold Walmart stock that the best person to run the company is you. It defies logic.

Here's another example: If I need a brain surgeon and your degree is in law, even if it's from an Ivy League school, you cannot help me. If you are a brain surgeon and I need help with beating charges for a crime I did not commit; you are of no use to me.

The importance of executive experience is that when you are in charge, stuff must get done. Governors can, will, and do argue with their opposition, but as executives, they must balance their budget, maintain the state infrastructure, and handle a hundred other pressing matters. They do not have the luxury of arguing endlessly. They must make sure stuff runs well. That prepares you for being President. Being a senator for five minutes does not.

Considering this, you may be wondering where I come down on the matter of our new President, Donald Trump, who had no political experience prior to running for office. In fact, you're probably burning to know the answer. Well, I will answer this question . . . later in the book, because it is not about President Trump, it is about Obama's eight years in office. But a bit of foreshadowing: Our new President met one of my qualifications for the executive office, though let's just say his run for the post held a morbid fascination as well.

But back to Obama. He simply hadn't amassed the skills necessary for the job he was aiming to get. It gives me no pleasure to say this now or in 2007 when he was running.

I do not hate myself as a black man. No conservative black person does. We want America to succeed, and we are hardwired to want a black person to succeed. When an African-American is one of only a few in any position, and you are black, it is more frustrating and painful to see them fail than it is for a white person.

Commander-in-Failure

I feel confident in saying that every black conservative in America who has ever spoken against President Obama would have loved—desperately—to see him have the presidency that Ronald Reagan or Bill Clinton achieved.

Yes, President Obama has a high IQ. Yes, he went to good schools. Yes, he appears to be a good father and husband. Yes, he can deliver a rousing and emotionally stirring speech. Iconic words and phrases like "Yes We Can" and "Hope and Change" catapulted him into the Oval Office.

Obama set the world on fire with his campaign. His speeches uplifted most and caused a few to pass out from political ecstasy. On election night, he got 99 percent of the black vote. He got white Republicans to switch and vote for him. He won the popular vote by more than ten million cast ballots. He captured 365 Electoral College votes.

Frankly, he dominated election night.

And for many blacks, he became an instant saint. Before he even stepped into the Oval Office and sat behind the Resolute desk that John F. Kennedy had first worked at in that storied room, they placed him on the same altar as Martin Luther King, Malcolm X, Marcus Garvey, and Nelson Mandela.

So how has Obama worked out for his worshippers?

Are African-Americans better off today than before he took office? Is America in a better place? How are the millions of white Republicans who put him in the office feeling about their vote in 2008? Has America moved into a post-racial time?

If you watch the news, these questions seem absurd. The hope and change Obama espoused did not come to pass. What happened? Obama had a mandate. He had the emotional heart of the nation. Blacks cried the night of his election, and so did many others.

Where did Obama's promise go and why?

It didn't go anywhere. Obama embodied the title of this book: He was a failure.

It's the "why" behind his lack of success that I will attempt to answer in *Failure*. The why provides lessons for future Presidents and leaders. It douses the fire of racial excuses and myths of Republican intransigence. It will tell the tale and do so from the view of Obama's natural constituency.

Obama's singular role in American history is because of his blackness. Make him white, and he would not have been elected President. His success and failures are different for the black community. The hopes, dreams, and expectations piled onto Obama by others of his race are different. His blackness made and makes being critical of him a cultural grenade.

If you are black, you were supposed to support President Obama. Being critical of him makes you the black sheep in the community—a racial and cultural pariah. Who wants to deal with that?

I certainly did not. But stark reality punched me dead in the face on election night 2008, and the years after have proved the feeling correct. I have no choice but to speak the truth about our first black President.

Our Commander-in-Failure.

CHAPTER ONE

OBAMACARE...
SIGNATURE DISASTER

Barack Obama could have been the greatest President in modern history.

That is not hyperbole. It is the net result of what Obama *could* have been, given the situation he walked into as President.

He entered office with 365 electoral college votes. He garnered over sixty-nine million votes in the popular vote, beating Senator John McCain by over ten million votes. More importantly, under the furious winds of the Obama election storm, the Democrats took the House of Representatives by 257 Congressmen to the Republicans' 178, and 57 Senate seats. Pouring salt into the wounds, Independents Joe Lieberman, who campaigned for McCain, and Bernie Sanders caucused with the Democrats regularly.

Obama was in full control. He had the House, the Senate, and with a post-election approval rating near seventy percent, he had the people. It could be easily said, and was quite often, that he had a mandate.

The pathway to anything on his agenda was wide open. The smart play would have been to laser-focus in on the economy. Even though exiting President George W. Bush had bullied TARP

(Troubled Asset Relief Fund) through, ostensibly to save the country from the mortgage meltdown, and Congress would push through a stimulus package in 2009, the economy was still weak. *Fragile* would have been a much better description.

Given that fact, for all the noise some Republicans made about the cost of the trillion-dollar Obama giveaway (conveniently forgetting their giveaway with TARP), there was little work needed from the Democrats or President Obama to get it passed. It was a typical Washington money-throw at a problem that did not expend any political capital. If ever there was a gimme in politics, the stimulus bill was it. If President Obama had decided to create and fund an infrastructure bank, increase the minimum wage to a "living wage," or go after companies that ship jobs overseas—which Donald Trump would do years later—he would have had a fight on his hands—a fight he may have been able to win. Instead, he set his eyes on a true legacy play, and ideological nirvana, in the form of reforming America's health care system.

Most Americans were not clamoring for Health care reform. The economy, the wars in Iraq and Afghanistan, and immigration reform were much higher priorities. But everyone is touched by health care. If you are not sick, then you know someone who is. Either you, a friend, or a family member has complained about the cost of health care. If you are not paying a hospital or medical bill, then you are most likely paying a health insurance premium for medical coverage. Health care expenses account for seventeen percent of the US gross national product (GDP). In real dollars, that is 3.8 trillion dollars annually.

Political historians and pundits may have thought it was a mistake to focus in on health care, but if you reform it—if you reform it correctly—you affect the life of EVERY SINGLE American citizen and do so for decades.

It cements your Presidency. As long you just do it right.

For Democrats, any conversation about health care started with the notion that health care insurance is a right; same as the right to free speech, gay marriage, or anything else in the Bill of Rights. They extrapolate all policy talk and decisions from that core belief. Even though there was a video floating around that showed President Obama's view that health care is a right, and his support ultimately for a single-payor solution in American, he decided to shift the focus. He moved the conversation away from health care as a right to a conversation about the core problems with the American health care system. The primary areas of concern were:

1.   The 46 million Americans without health insurance.

2.   The sad stories of families bankrupted because of medical costs that hospitals charged and that exceeded the cost caps from their insurance plans.

3.   The high cost of health care premiums for Americans.

4.   The degree to which medicals costs added to the US deficit.

These four areas formed the basis for Obama's push, and campaign to begin health care reform. In every speech, interview, or press release, President Obama pressed those issues repeatedly. It was a brilliant political move, because everyone, including Republicans, knew that all four were problems that people wanted to have fixed. Republicans geared up for a fight. They knew that whatever plan the Democrats created, it would be government-centered. It did not matter. The Republicans were in no position to fight. Obama had won the election decisively. He also stole the emotional center of the issue. He had the high ground.

He protected that high ground with a wall made of heartstring-pulling ideas, such as: keeping children on their parent's insurance longer, no benefit caps, and the big one, no pre-existing conditions.

After months of secret meetings, high-tension acrimony with Republicans, arm-twisting of Blue-Dog democrats, and tremendous expending of political capital, the Affordable Care Act, known colloquially as Obamacare, was passed into law. It was a 900-page monstrosity that completely remade the American health care and insurance systems.

It was a significant accomplishment. Big enough to make Vice-President Joe Biden whisper into President Obama's ear, a little too loudly, before he signed it into law, "this is a big fucking deal..." The Affordable Care Act would become his signature program.

It would also become his biggest self-inflicted wound.

I come at this whole subject from a unique point of view. Unlike political pundits, radio hosts, or even congressman arguing for or against Obamacare, I know the health care field intimately. I spent fifteen years as a financial advisor and health insurance agent. I have sat at the kitchen tables of real Americans, helping them map out the best and most affordable health insurance for their family. I have taken the calls from sick or hospitalized clients who need to make sure their policies cover the expenses of their medical emergency. I have called in the claims, and have sat down to deliver the bad news when a client has a health care expense that is not covered. Sometimes it is because it is not a covered procedure, sometimes because they reached a cost limit in the policy, but most often it was because it was a health expense they chose not to cover when we were constructing the policy.

I'm an expert in the health insurance field, and at the level it matters most; in the lives of the people it covers. When you are an insurance agent, it is your job to know how all policies work, how they pay, and what they do not pay. I have studied the pricing, the underwriting, and actuarial variables. It is your responsibility—one I took seriously—to advise families on which coverage options are best, needed, not needed, and how to find one that fits their family budget. As an agent or financial adviser, there is no policy type you have not seen. There is no exception, coverage, or rider you do not know about. The critical thing, however, is that you know how regulations and certain policy choices affect pricing.

Individuals like Dr. Ezekiel Emmanuel or Jonathan Gruber can bandy about as health insurance experts, but they have never had to sit down with a real family to shop options on health coverage. They have never gotten a claim call in the middle of the night, nor sat down with a family and explained why they need one coverage type versus another. I have done this. So have millions of other financial advisors and insurance agents. We understand what makes the price of a health insurance policy rise or fall in a way no college professor, policy wonk, or elected official can.

When the details of the law were constructed, there were a lot of politicians in the room. There were plenty of researchers, statisticians, professors, regulators, health care interest groups, and of course a few health insurers. Do you know who was missing?

No underwriters—the people who know the risks of each medical ailment.

No actuaries—the people who do the high-level math and know the costs of each risk and the pricing elements of every type of possible policy/benefit configuration.

No insurances agents or financial advisers—the people who see the real-world effects of insurance on people, and who are responsible for knowing a good deal of the information that the two groups above know.

You cannot construct a workable health care reform without those people in the room. But what does workable mean? The problems and challenges surrounding health care are, for the most part, agreed upon. No one doubted the problems that President Obama insisted Obamacare would solve, were, in fact, problems that needed solving. The issue has always been: How do you solve those agreed-upon problems?

Many Democrats think health care and health insurance are the same things. In their minds, if you have health insurance, you have health care. Second, those same Democrats believe that medical costs are expensive because insurance companies are greedy. They charge too much and try to get out of paying. In their minds, if you are making a profit, then there is no way you can be trusted to do the right thing. It is an attitude we see from Democrats regarding financial services, education, and energy to name a few. Therefore, the only way to lower the costs of health care in a Democrat's mind is to put the government in control of it.

Conversely, many Republicans see the lack of competition as the primary problem. In each state, there are only a few health insurers—five or six at a maximum, which means there is little competition. No competition means higher prices, no matter what is sold. Republicans have, for years, wanted to open health insurance to be bought and sold across state lines. Car insurance is sold in this manner, and is why you can get a policy that does not blow a hole in your monthly budget.

Per the American Health Insurance Plans (AHIP), there are 1300 health plans in total throughout the country. Because you cannot buy across state lines, you do not have access to all 1300 plans. You only have access to the ones in your state and area. For example, I once sold a policy to a client in Jacksonville, Florida that was $450 per month, but the same type of policy in Tennessee was $187.00. Why the difference?

Each state has a department that regulates the insurance industry. Most of these insurance regulators do not want the state lines to be opened. Further, each state has health insurance mandates, items that must be covered that other states might not require. The more you must cover in a policy, the more expensive it will be. Further, there is no discretion as to whether it is a coverage item that a person needs. What this all means in policy terms, however, is that Republicans believe a factor in keeping the costs high is the amount of government involvement in the industry.

Republicans also point to lawsuits as another reason medical costs are so high. It is important to understand that health insurance *pays* for the medical costs. Insurance companies do not *create* the medical costs—doctors, clinics, and hospitals do that. All three get sued on a regular basis. Many of these lawsuits are legitimate. The number of deaths caused by medical mistakes ranks only third behind cancer and heart disease. Nonetheless, there are also lawsuits that are frivolous. Both types of lawsuits, as well as malpractice insurance, are factored into the costs of bills from hospitals. They are also the reason hospitals do so many tests. They want to try and protect themselves from liability as much as possible. This leads to a simple equation. The more tests you have, the more expensive your bill.

In general, these are the positions of each side. One wants the government to solve the problem. The other wants to move government out of the way a bit and let market forces do their work. Regardless of which side you believe, the policy prescriptions are vastly different from one side to the other.

One constant narrative, and it endures even today, is that the Republicans would not work with the President. They had no ideas and did not want to compromise. This was a false narrative. President Obama decided to ignore completely any ideas from the Republicans. He shut them out of the discussions. In one meeting he had, a televised health summit, he told Sen. John McCain, "The election is over, John." In other words, "I won. Go into the corner and remain silent."

He also did not think he needed their input. He had the majority. He could pass whatever he liked, if all Democrats followed him. Most laws do not get passed without votes from the opposite party. If you manage to force it through without bi-partisan support, it usually does not stay law. Historically, that is the truth, but President Obama ignored that history lesson. If instead he had heeded it, he could have been the most successful President ever.

I want you to understand that it is at that moment, with those words to Sen. McCain and the Republicans at the summit, that the seeds of Obama's presidency began to unravel. The moment he shut them out, his chance at being a great president died.

He made two critical mistakes.

First, he allowed hubris to get the better of him and of the Democratic Party. Yes, he had the numbers. He had the votes in Congress. He had the popularity. He also had a bunch of concepts the public liked. No American likes to see someone lose everything because a child is sick. No American wants a loved one refused health care because they are already sick. Americans are big-hearted, and feel for the people who cannot get or do not have health insurance. EVERYONE wants to pay a lower premium. Further, the public all agreed with the general goals of health care reform, even if they did not understand how to get to those goals.

But Americans also want to see their leaders work together. They are in fact, used to it. Reagan worked with a Democratic congress his entire term. Bill Clinton lost the House and Senate, had epic fights with Newt Gingrich, and still passed many bills and laws with them. George W. Bush did not start the Iraq war on a word alone. A bucket-load of Democrats voted for him. By shutting the Republicans out, Obama was setting up opposition he did not need and could have curtailed. It is easy to vote against and fight a law that has nothing you want in the bill.

The second problem he created is that he went big, instead of focusing on the core problems. All President Obama had to do was focus on the following things:

- Do away with health expense caps
- Allow kids to stay on coverage to age 25
- Get rid of pre-existing conditions
- Allow purchases across state lines
- Make insurance affordable for the 45 million people who did not have it
- A form of minor lawsuit reform

That's all he had to do. Three items on this list are so popular; Republicans would have been forced to accept them. If you need proof of that, consider that the Republican *Repeal and Replace* plan leaves those three items in place.

This list would have altered the problem of cost, kept the basic things Democrats and the public wanted, and forced the Republicans into voting for it without a strong fight. He could have forced their compliance, for lack of a better term, while looking like a true leader.

It was simple. It was easy-breezy. Instead, Obama went another direction that led to a major fight in Congress, no Republican support, and began to wake up a large part of the electorate that had slept through the McCain campaign.

And for what?

THE PROBLEM WITH OBAMACARE

Even before the complete law was finalized and released to the public, leaks and public campaigns by President Obama and his surrogates revealed many of the broad strokes. Proposed provisions like allowing children to stay on their parent's plans until age twenty-six was a benefit I found to be silly. As an early-age adult, I found health insurance without my parents. As far as I am concerned, any child—including yours—can find coverage on their own. Unless they are in school, there is no reason to continue to treat your adult child as a five-year-old. Other provisions, like removing the cap on medical expenses, I understood emotionally, but like most people who understood insurance, I knew it would increase the cost. My experience also showed me that an unlimited cap was unnecessary. Raising them from two million to, say, five million, could accomplish the same goal—providing families with an extra blanket of protection against rare, large-scale medical expenses.

Nonetheless, I kept my ultimate opinion unformed. I had learned in the insurance field that rumors from managers or marketing reps about changes to insurance benefits or compensation meant nothing until you saw the facts in writing. I applied the same mindset to the future health care reform.

In March of 2010, the Obama Administration released the full text of the health care reform for public comment. Until it was released, no one knew how large the bill was. It turned out to be nine-hundred pages long. Most members of Congress—Republican and Democrat alike—had not seen a single line of the bill until it was released. The administration gave both Congress and the public two weeks to peruse the law and make comments regarding it before a vote would be held.

I want you to pause, regardless of your political affiliation and mindset, and think about that for a moment. You have two weeks, that's fourteen days, to study nine hundred pages.

~pause~ while Jeopardy music plays in your head

Even if you want health care reform, event if you are a ride-or-die Barack Obama supporter, you know you cannot possibly read, let alone study a law that long and complicated in just fourteen days. It's a joke. The public was expected to accept, and members of Congress to vote, "yea" or "nay" on something they could not possibly understand.

In my mind, the outcome, the law's passage was a foregone conclusion. The behind-closed-doors meetings shut out Republican lawmakers from the planning, and the exposed arm-twisting of Blue Dog Democrats made it clear that public comment or changes because of them would not be forthcoming. Obama had decided. He had the numbers; he was going to do what the hell he wanted.

Nonetheless, I downloaded the entire law onto my desktop and preceded to do what 90 percent of Americans did not do, what only 50 percent of law makers would end up doing, and what I know to this day Barack Obama never did; I read the entire law. Every page, every twisted line of legalese. It took me three months, and a boatload of teasing jokes from friends, of the "get a life" variety

19

to complete it. I did not stop there; could not even if I wanted to. The language of the law is too tortured to understand in spots. I supplemented my reading with briefs written by law firms and articles from the Kaiser Foundation. I kept my reading to pieces that explained what was in the law, not an opinion about the law.

Bluntly, I did President Obama's job. I did the job he did not do. What the law, as written, coupled with my *expert* experience in insurance, told me was simple.

Obamacare could not work.

This has nothing to do with the President. It had nothing to do with the differences between a Liberal or Conservative worldview. It was all about structure.

Let's review the goals again: *Lower health insurance premiums, not adding to the national deficit, covering the 45 million Americans without health insurance, reducing overall medical costs.* Goals worthy to be pursued. However, the law as written made it structurally impossible to obtain those goals.

Obamacare's foundation begins with a set of beliefs. The highlighted benefits are/were: no pre-existing conditions, no medical cost limits, and children on their parents plan to age 26. Adding to that list was a set of mandates that all insurance companies would have to adhere to. In other words, the government would not take over the health care system—insurance companies would still exist—but they were told what they had to cover. These mandates were in the following general areas:

- Ambulatory Services
- Emergency Services
- Hospitalization
- Maternity and Newborn care

- Mental health and substance abuse disorders
- Prescriptions Drugs
- Rehabilitation services
- Lab services
- Prevention and wellness services
- Chronic disease Management
- Pediatric services
- Limit total out-of-pocket spending amounts chosen by government
- Limit the age and who could buy so-called *catastrophic* health policies

To the public, none of those items seem like bad things. Show the list to anyone, even a die-hard Obama critic, and they will agree those are legitimate medical expenses. So, what's the issue?

Well, the devil is in the details. The mandates direct what each and every single policy sold had to cover. Let me illuminate this with an example. As an insurance agent, when I sat down with a single, young, male business owner, I would have been sanctioned by insurance regulators if I sold him pediatric coverage. Why? Because he does not have kids. He does not need coverage for kids.

Here is another example, a personal one. I am not an alcoholic, nor do I take drugs. Therefore, I do not need to buy a policy that covers drug treatment or rehab. I can put the cost savings of not having that coverage into something else, like gas in my car.

Preventive services are a great concept. If you can prevent heart disease, you not only save lives, you reduce the overall costs dedicated to dealing with the aftermath of getting heart disease. This is a concept that health care researchers and President Obama pushed hard in speeches, but that's not the type of preventive services Obamacare mandates. It mandates coverage for preventive care (which, by the way, 99 percent of all private insurance plans already covered at little to no cost) and preventive practices like... acupuncture, reiki, and other alternative services.

In line with preventive services is coverage for prescriptions. Drugs should be covered, but in perhaps in the biggest example of an unnecessary liberal giveaway, coverage for birth control, AT NO COST, was mandated[1]. A great deal of hay was made about this regulation, including several cases that would make it to the Supreme Court regarding the company Hobby Lobby and the Little Sisters of the Poor. The usual accusations of sexism and rhetoric about women's health were bandied about. Let me cut through all of that for you.

Ninety-nine percent of all health insurance plans in America already covered birth control. There was no crisis of coverage for drugs, or devices to prevent unplanned pregnancies. That is a fact. The only thing that differed from plan to plan and prescription to prescription were the out-of-pocket costs. Birth Control pills usually cost between a ten-dollar and twenty-five dollar co-pay. The rest was covered by the insurance plan. IUD's were usually covered at a twenty to thirty percent of the cost co-insurance. Simply put, co-pays for the cost of birth control were not sending single American women into the poor house. But now, every birth control method would be free of charge.

The problem with mandating that every plan includes it and at no cost is simple. This increases the cost structure of any insurance plan. Nothing is free. If you do not pay for something, the cost must be obtained from someplace. In insurance, if the plan is going to cover a health care expense, you pay a premium for that privilege.

---

1 This provision was actually as via regulation, allowing it to by-pass scrutiny on the front side

The more expenses covered, the more the company must pay out, the higher your monthly premiums. By requiring each insurance plan to cover birth control at no cost to individuals, the cost has to go up. Also, we go back to the pediatric example. What man needs coverage for birth control pills on his plan? If a woman is past childbearing age, why does she need this coverage?

Look, let me explain this like I would if I was at your kitchen table, selling a health insurance policy. Deductibles and co-pays are designed to keep the cost of your monthly premium down. All other things being equal, a health policy with a five-thousand-dollar deductible will have a lower monthly premium than a plan with only a twenty-five-hundred-dollar deductible. It is better to pay a small amount for certain services to keep your costs low. Despite protestations of people like Sandra Fluke, who believe there are women who cannot put food on the table because of birth control costs, there is not a single woman in America that cannot afford a ten or twenty-dollar co-payment for her birth control.

Do not agree? Consider this, how many women do you know who do the following:

1. Get their hair done
2. Buy shoes
3. Get pedicures or manicures
4. Have a smart phone
5. Have a cell phone plan
6. Smoke
7. Drink coffee

These items all cost more than twenty dollars each month. Therefore, they can afford to pay a co-payment. Besides, when it comes to sex, men are imbeciles. If a woman is willing to give us some, she can basically get him to do anything. Making him spend eights bucks on a family pack of condoms is a breeze.

Ten or twenty dollars is not a lot of money, but when you magnify that across 150 million people or more, that is a significant cost to tack on the system you are trying to sell as going to be a cheaper option.

Leave the politics or social beliefs on the side. Always go back to the main goal. Lower the cost of health insurance premiums, so more people can afford to buy insurance. How can you do that if you are adding to the cost structure of the plans? If you believe that birth control free-of-charge is necessary, fine, that is one argument. But if your goal is to lower the cost of insurance, you cannot do that by adding coverage items.

As I studied the primary structure of the Obamacare law, it became clear that the law had been turned into an ideological and political wish list, not a law focused on solving a problem. For example, another mandate is the prohibition against women having a higher monthly premium than a man of the same age and health status. The Democrats considered this discriminatory practice. It shows a lack of understanding of what insurance is about.

Insurance is a balance between risk and costs. What an insurance company is doing when it prices a policy is to look at the associated risk of paying out claims for certain events and the income—or monthly premium—that will be needed to cover these expenses. These risks are quantifiable and measurable. Part of the equation is the risk pool at which you are looking. That's a fancy word for examining the groups: people, age group, occupation, etc. and their risk/cost factors.

Take automobile insurance as an example. If a man and woman are the same age, same driving record, the same type of car… the man's premium will be higher. Why? Because men are riskier drivers. We drive faster; we have more accidents than women, we are more prone to drinking and driving than women, we drive aggressively; we cost insurance companies more money. Therefore, in general, car insurance premiums are higher for men than for women.

It is the exact opposite in health insurance. Women have annual physicals they must get; they have babies, they have complications from having babies, they live longer, and so have a longer tail of medical costs. They cost insurance companies more money. This is an objective fact. It can be found in any government report that shows a breakdown of male versus female expenses.

That means the risk of a higher medical expense payout is higher for coverage of women than for men. Higher risk means a higher premium. It is not discrimination. It is basic math—and common sense, I will add.

Now, you may think a woman's premium being higher than a man having the same age, health factors, etc. is discriminatory. I may disagree because of my experience in the field, but neither of those things matters. What matters is that by requiring level premiums, you are curtailing the income needed by the insurance company to offset higher costs properly. That means high premiums for everyone.

Two other mandates further compounded this problem. The first being that all employers with more than 50 employees working more than 30 hours a week had to provide coverage. That coverage had to include what was called the *minimum plan thresholds*. Essentially, the plans offered to the employees had to cover all the items listed above. So the number of people who were going to be covered would rise, and the level of coverage they were being given had to meet the minimum requirements.

Think of this analogy. If you have ten children in your family, and you need to buy one a car, that is one type of expense. If, however, you are told you must buy a car for all ten kids, and that car must be a Mercedes, then that is a whole different type of expense.

It does not matter if giving everyone a car of the same type is fair or not. Doing so changes your cost structure dramatically.

In insurance, the only way to alleviate that problem is the rule of large numbers and deductibles. The law of large numbers is simply a concept where if you spread the risk of any expense among a large group, the cost per person goes down. Deductibles and co-pays, on the other hand, create lower premiums because the insurance holder is shouldering more of the medical costs. When part of the medical costs is shared, it allows the insurance company to offer a lower premium.

Obamacare does not help in that area either. Risk and cost... those are things that matter. If you are a lower risk, and you are willing to pick up the cost for something, then your rate is lower. Imagine a young person or well-paid young adult who is healthy. They are not a high health risk. On an average basis, they get sick a few times year, and that's it. Further, if they are well-paid, or have some resources, they can afford a higher deductible. People in this life circumstance will often choose a Catastrophic plan—plans that used to be called major medical. Basically, they are willing to take a $10,000 deductible to protect themselves against something truly tragic, but who needs a health policy to see a doctor about the flu?

However, in the Obamacare law, there is a limit on who can buy these types of plans. Only people who are age twenty-five and younger and make less than $50,000 can buy these plans. If you are thirty and make seventy-five thousand dollars a year, you are prohibited from having this type of plan.

On the deductible front, Obamacare created four plans. All plans are the same, by the way. A bronze plan with Aetna is the same plan as a bronze plan with Humana. The plan that has the lower premium has a higher deductible and higher out-of-pocket costs. Those costs are higher than what a low-income person can afford. Think about this. If you could not afford health insurance before, how can you afford the Obamacare plan now, which has higher out-of-pocket costs?

Isn't the cost of health insurance the problem Obamacare was going to fix?

Obamacare is a complicated law. There are twists, turns, roundabouts, and contingencies in hundreds of areas. Explaining every detail would take two or three 400-plus-page books. I am not going to do that to you here. We do not have enough room. What I am trying to show with these examples is this: By looking at the issue ideologically, the people who put the law together compromised the end goal. You cannot possibly add more expenses to be covered, limit the number of people who can buy plans that limit their costs to only big ticket items, AND increase the number of people covered without affecting the cost structure of the insurance plan upward. It is not possible. You can make an argument about wanting these benefits, or how fair they are to everyone or some other argument for their adoption, but those are value propositions. They have nothing to do with cost, which is a black and white issue. It is basic math. Higher-cost items cost you more money. So what were these people in the back rooms doing? Are they just stupid?

The answer is no.

Nancy Pelosi, Harry Reid, and the people behind the law knew they had to find a way to handle the costs involved in health care reform—both practically and politically. The solution they decided upon comprised three major political gimmicks, the first being the most controversial—health care coverage would become a mandated product for people to buy.

BUY WHAT I TELL YOU TO OR ELSE

As an American, there are certain rights you have as your birthright. You have freedom of speech. You can call President Bush a stupid monkey; you can call Nancy Pelosi a hag. If you choose, you can say Barack Obama is a traitorous Muslim. You can say those things, and more, without the government being able to do a thing about it.

You have the freedom to be in any religion you choose. Join a mosque, a synagogue, or become a monk. You decide, it is your choice. There is not a damn thing the government can do about it.

In addition to those rights that you receive as an American, you were now going to be given something else, a mandatory health insurance bill. Ostensibly, the framers of Obamacare would say that the government has the right and power to do this under the Commerce Clause. The text of the commerce clause reads as follows:

> "...which gives Congress the power to regulate commerce with foreign nations, and among the several states, and with the Indian tribes."

That sentence means Congress can regulate what you buy; it does not say Congress has the power to force you to buy anything.

Obamacare is flatly unconstitutional.

Yes, I know the Supreme Court, per Justice Roberts, says that it's constitutional. But with all due respect to the Justice's years on the bench, it does not take a law degree and years as a lawyer to understand the Constitution. It only takes a seventh-grade reading level and five minutes on Google. The Constitution is written in plainer English than the Affordable Care Act. I know, I have read both more than once. In no sentence does the Constitution tell citizens the government can force them to buy a product, and specifically the product that the government tells you to buy. Congress cannot tell you to buy a smart car instead of an SUV. It cannot tell you to put windmills in your backyard instead of a generator. Congress cannot say murders in South Side Chicago are too high, so every resident must buy an AR-15, and if you do not, we are going to penalize you.

The Rush Limbaughs and Sean Hannitys of the world will tell you the Democrats did this because they crave power. I have always found that to be off the mark. Democrats do not crave power; they just like to use it to force people to do what they want. If they think something is bad, they want to make you stop doing it. If they think something is good, then they want to force you to do it. It is that simple.

In the case of Obamacare, however, the prevailing need to force all Americans into a plan is because you need millions of people in the system to spread out the costs. Without everyone signing up, the rule of large numbers will not work in your favor.

Imagine it like this—let's say you have two college students who are hungry. They want to go out to eat, but the restaurant they are going to charges ten dollars for a chicken dinner. One student has seven dollars; the other has only five. Neither can afford a plate. However, if they go to the manager and say, "Hey, if you reduce the cost of the chicken plate to seven dollars, I can get ten other students to come in and eat right now." The manager would be inclined to accept the deal because he is getting more business. The students can eat out now because the cost is lower since a larger number of people are coming to eat. That is a simplified example of how the spreading of risk and costs among many people works in insurance. If you have a large enough pool, the costs can remain low. If you do not have a large number, you cannot get the price down.

Using the dinner example, here is how this would look. If the student can only get five extra people to come to the restaurant his deal with the manager does not work out. Further, imagine he does get the extra ten people, but instead of ordering chicken, they all order lobster or steak. There is no way to keep the dinners at ten dollars each because everyone ordered more expensive food. This is what happened with Obamacare. They added a bunch of lobster and steak to your dinner, told you that you had to eat it, and then said they would charge a fee to anyone who did not show up for dinner anyway.

The second gimmick was an expansion of the Medicaid system. Under Obamacare, the income levels for who could qualify for Medicaid expanded. This matters as it relates to the budget for Obamacare. One of the promises was that the law would be deficit-neutral, meaning the law would not add to the national deficit. Medicaid is a state program. On the front end, Medicaid expenses are not included in the budget of any law. Of course, the federal government sends Medicaid funding to the states as grants on the back-end, but as a budget matter, the expenses are not included.

By expanding the Medicaid rolls, President Obama could say more people had health care and shifted the expenses away from the

Obamacare law on the front end. That makes it look less expensive than it is.

However, there was a problem. The regulations did not just enlarge the pool of people who could qualify for Medicaid; it mandated they take Medicaid. This is why many Americans lost their doctors. They were moved into Medicaid, and their doctors did not take Medicaid. Their only option was to buy a private plan under Obamacare, but they would not be able to receive a subsidy to lower the cost; which was the third gimmick they used.

If I had a dollar for every time President Obama said, "The cost of health insurance plans will go down, and be more affordable for families," I would have more money than Donald Trump. It was a fantasy at best, a blatant lie at worst. But the appearance of lower costs to individuals could be given, vis-a-vis a government subsidy, better known as a welfare payment. Using fines, fees, and new taxes contained throughout the Obamacare law to generate new revenue, the government would use some of it to pay a portion of American's insurance premiums. For example, as a single person living in New York with no kids, and an annual income of $30,000, a plan under Obamacare would be $456 per month[2]. However, I am eligible for a subsidy from the government of $249.00. So, I only pay roughly half. If I am married with two kids and have a $45,000 yearly income, then I get a subsidy of around $872, and only pay around $270 a month in premiums.

This is a common governmental scheme. Pay a portion of the costs, so that the end user—the American citizen—does not feel the pain. If a person is shielded from the true cost, you can claim you are lowering the cost of their health insurance. In reality, you

---

2 http://kff.org/interactive/subsidy-calculator/

are not. You are just shifting where the payment for coverage is going to come from. Now, perhaps you are a person who believes the government should handle the costs of health care insurance. That is one debate. But, the goal, or one of them, was to lower the cost of medical expenses to the national budget. You cannot do that if you are creating a new entitlement program that is doling out money.

It does not matter whether you think they should. That is a different debate, a different argument. What matters here is the goal of lowering costs. Giving money out to people, even if you think they need it, does not lower costs.

In the aftermath of the law's passage, I wrote several articles, and I was a guest on a few talk radio shows, discussing the problems with the law. I always focused on the structural issues with Obamacare—its nuts and bolts as it related to medical and premiums costs. I never delved into how I felt emotionally about it, but that feeling was one of grinding frustration—frustration with Obama for making something simple into something complicated. Annoyance with the wasted opportunity because he could not just get out of his own ideological way. Total and complete exasperation from fellow black people who supported the law and had no clue what it was going to do to black people.

Blacks were cheering across with the country when Obama signed ACA into law, without realizing—in truth not wanting to know—how negatively the law would affect their communities. It is no surprise to most people that as a group, African-Americans have an average income lower than the average white American. In 2014 the Pew Research Center found that the median income for a white household was $71,000, as compared to blacks at $43,000.[3] The poverty rate for blacks is at 36 percent, with most of that number made up of households with a single black female as the parent and sole income provider. That is an average; drill down into the urban centers where black populations are concentrated, and that number gets higher. On the surface, it is a poster-child situation for why Obamacare and its subsidies are needed.

Keep drilling, and the truth is revealed as something different. Take President Obama's adopted home of Chicago for example. The average income in Chicago is $35,000. That is an average, so we can surmise that a single person without a college degree living in the black neighborhoods of South Side is lower. How much lower is a guess. People like to lump South Side into one area, but it is not. It has neighborhoods that are considered nice and not welfare-ridden or crime-prone. For the sake of argument, let's choose $30,000 as a number. It is under the average, but just outside the eligibility level for Illinois state Medicaid. In other terms, it is the Obamacare sweet spot.

If you go to the Kaiser Center, you can find a calculator that will estimate the subsidy anyone can get across the country for Obamacare. In Chicago, our single black female with two kids would get $423 a month, leaving her a payment of only $100 per month for health insurance. On the south side of Chicago, the average rent is $800-$900 per month. Then there would be utilities, phone, gas and a car payment if you have a car, and transportation costs if you do not. I will let you decide whether $100 per month after expenses and with two kids, deserves the moniker of "only."

_____

3 http://www.pewsocialtrends.org/2016/06/27/on-views-of-race-and-inequality-blacks-and-whites-are-worlds-apart/

Here is the wrinkle. Remember that pesky employer mandate? If our single black female has an income of 30k a year, she is not sitting around collecting welfare. She is working, and if her employer has more than 50 employees, they must offer her insurance. If her employer offers health insurance, our single black female is not eligible for subsidies. Why would she need Obamacare, if she can get coverage from her employer? Her plan at work might be too expensive; it may meet the minimum requirements, but is not a comprehensive plan. In the aftermath of Obamacare's passage, plans of this type exploded, because they are lower cost to the employer. If she wants Obamacare or needs it because she needs good coverage, she can get it. She just has to pay $523 per month for it.

How is her monthly budget looking now?

This is a problem Americans of all races are facing, but if you are in a group that has less income than others, it hits you harder. Millions of blacks are part of the working poor. They were part of that 45-million-people group without insurance, and now many still could not get it. They did not qualify for subsidies, and they cannot afford the premiums without them.

Once again, a Democrat had promised blacks something, and it was not going to come true. That the person making the promise was also black was salt in the wound. In truth, it is a wound that would have salt applied to it over and over again. The president did not promise blacks, specifically, their costs would go down. He promised that to everyone. Implicit in the rhetoric, however, was an emphasis on the poor and working class, which included many blacks.

Middle-class blacks got the same treatment. I have a good friend who shared their premium increase with me. Before Obamacare, they were paying $450 per month. After Obamacare, that shot up to $1500.

This brings me back to the primary cause of my frustration with Obama. He wasted a perfect freakin' opportunity because he had to be ideological. He had chosen to add political and social goodies to his health care plans as must-haves; he changed the system for everyone, rather than focusing on closing the gap for the 45 million who could not afford insurance. The bottom line is that 80 percent of Americans had insurance already when he showed up. They had it, and they were happy with it. They did not need these "necessary" new benefits, but he gave it to them anyway, mandating their inclusion into all insurance plans. Thus, he had to also mandate getting Obamacare. If Obamacare was going to work at all, it needed every American to sign up for it, it needed the added taxes contained in it and had to have the penalties for not signing up.

It was a financial Jenga block. As long as you had the right blocks in the right places, it would stand just fine. Remove one block, and it all collapses.

Doing it in this way guaranteed unnecessary blow back. You were not going to increase taxes by billions a year and not have Republicans fight it tooth and nail. You were not, ARE NOT, going to force Americans to buy anything without a harsh consequence. That consequence for Obama was the tea party, and crushing defeats in the 2010 mid-terms elections, followed by more losses in 2012.

More critical is that you cannot make something more expensive and expect Americans to buy it. That is the ultimate legacy and instrument of Obamacare's future defeat. After six years in existence, the results are in and recorded. Insurance premiums are higher now than before Obamacare. These are not the usual increases. Three months before the 2016 elections, news outlets began reporting increases of 22 percent on average for Obamacare premiums. Arizona saw the highest increase, moving up 116 percent[4].

Democrats tried—as they had previously—to blame the insurance companies, but the insurance industry pushed back by releasing the numbers. They showed a clear explanation. Medical payouts were higher than predicted or anticipated, and the number of people needed to sign up had not matched up. The premiums they had charged were not adequate to cover the medical claims paid out. Further, many states had insurers dropping out of the exchanges, and Obamacare plans altogether. Some states were down to just one or two insurance companies selling the Obamacare plans.

Every prediction about Obamacare made before it even began selling was coming true. In one interview I did, I started the interview with the words, "I told you so." The host responded with, "Yes, you did."

Republicans have tried to repeal Obamacare 30 different times. Of course, every attempt failed. You cannot get rid of the law the man at the head of the table has bet his legacy on—especially when you only have one part of the government. The Republicans needed to have not even bothered. The weight of all the mistakes in the law is bringing it down. It is obvious to everyone it needs to be reconstructed. Democrats pay lip service to "tweaking or fixing some aspects" of a law they said was perfect a scant six years ago, but they know it must be overhauled.

---

4 http://www.thefiscaltimes.com/2016/11/01/Here-s-How-Much-Obamacare-Premiums-Are-Rising-All-50-States

The ironic twist is that when you get a democrat who knows the law and is honest, they'll tell you they should keep all the provisions I laid out in the beginning as the main things they need to keep. Makes you wonder, "what if they had done it right the first time around?"

There is an old saying in the contracting and building industry: "Measure twice, cut once." The moral of the lesson being focus on what matters; measure your board to the correct length, and then double-check it. That way you get the right size the first time you make the cut.

Some supporters constantly yell, "At least he did something!" It's the most inane and dumb basis for an argument. Doing something—doing anything—does not matter when it's the wrong thing to do.

President Obama focused in on the wrong thing. Lowering the cost of insurance was what was needed. They did not need acupuncture or free birth control. Americans did not need to limit what insurance companies made from premiums, or even have their kids to be on the parental teat until age twenty-six. They needed their health care insurance premiums to be lower. They needed to be able to get insurance and afford the insurance they got.

President Obama did not give Americans what they needed. He gave them what he wanted them to have.

And that is why he failed.

CHAPTER TWO

MESSAGE TO ALL POLITICIANS…
IT'S THE ECONOMY, STUPID

During the 2008 election and period immediately afterward, the number one concern for Americans was the economy. In a poll conducted two weeks after President Obama's inauguration, Gallup[5] found that fixing the economy was considered extremely important by 89 percent of the respondents. In addition, 41 percent of respondents considered it important.

Considering the events immediately before the election, this can hardly be surprising. After steady growth for years, and a stock market record of 11,000 on the Dow, the market took a tumble. The so-called "mortgage meltdown" began, and the housing bubble burst. In September 2008, the Dow dropped 778 points—the worst single-day drop since Black Monday in 1987. If not for safeguards in place to halt the market, the drop could have been worse.

The drop was a signal—a leak that preceded the dam breaking. In two months, the Dow went from a record high of 11,000 down to 8046 points. The almost three-thousand-point drop represented billions in lost wealth, retirement plans, and stockholder equity.

---

5 http://www.gallup.com/poll/104320/iraq-economy-top-is-sues-voters.aspx

Commander-in-Failure

Stock market perennial Bear Sterns shut down permanently. My former employer, and investment house granddaddy, Merrill Lynch, would disappear, being absorbed into Bank of America. Massive lay-offs ensued as the money that flowed through the economy dried up. President George Bush was being told that the country's whole financial system and the economy could collapse. Most Americans were in a panic. We were facing a modern depression.

At least that is what everyone was saying. And by everyone, I mean, politicians, academics, and a certain Presidential candidate named Barack Obama. The economic downturn, created by the sub-prime mortgage market, played right into the hands of his candidacy. People forget that just before the events began to unfold, McCain had taken a slight lead in the polls. The pop in the mortgage bubble placed a permanent pop in Senator McCain's presidential hopes.

Presidents get the blame and praise for events that happen when they are in office, whether it is fair or not. President Bush got the blame for the mortgage crisis and the subsequent recession that followed. In all, the crisis cost America 9 million jobs. It lost about 40 percent of its previous GDP growth.

In truth, the event had little to do with President Bush. The catalyst for the mortgage meltdown was Fannie Mae and Freddie Mac. For years, in part because of Bill Clinton's affordable housing effort in the 90's, Fannie and Freddie forced banks to lend to risky homebuyers. To be sure, the private lending market had its own amount of blame for the situation, but the beginning lay at the doorstep of the two federally-backed mortgage insurers. President Bush tried 22 different times to reform and rein in both agencies. A simple YouTube[6] search will show videos of dozens of hearings and the democrats to anyone who cares to look—led by members of the Congressional Black Caucus members—blocking each attempt. As far as they were concerned, Fannie Mae and Freddie Mac were just fine.

Unpacking the cause of the sub-prime market is outside the scope of this book. There are dozens of books that have examined the subject down to its molecular parts, explaining in detail what I just asserted above. The best of the bunch is _Shaky Ground_, by Bethany McLean. But, regardless of the cause, it did happen, and America went into recession. Barack Obama was elected, and one of the things he was supposed to do is get the economy growing again. Get people into good paying jobs.

A great deal, especially from President Obama himself, has been made about the hand he was dealt. Most democrats consider it the "worst economy since the Great Depression." That is the mantra spoken again and again. This is important to note because it allows and has allowed President Obama to claim more success with his stewardship of the economy than he would be given if people thought the recession was an average one.

To be sure, it was not. Unemployment did rise to a peak of 10.5 percent. America lost 40 percent of the country's GDP growth. Anyone thinking about retiring in 2009 could not do it. The stock market had plummeted to 8046, most 401(k) retirement plans were decimated. The country was in a severe economic crunch. Uncertainty was a real feeling for the working and moneyed classes alike. Worse, many of the former Bush cabinet members, journalists,

---

6 https://www.youtube.com/watch?v=IyqYY72PeRM

and politicians frightened people into thinking that America was facing another depression.

However, Ronald Reagan had a direr situation to deal with when he took office. After four years of President Carter, the unemployment rate was 8.5 percent[7]. This is below the peak of 10.5 percent at the start of President Obama's term, but is worse when considering that in the Seventies, most Americans were in one-income households. Interest rates rose to a peak of 21 percent; inflation grew to 13.2 percent[8]. Americans were spending more time in gas lines than driving to work. Calling the economic conditions bad is an understatement. More important, they were worse than the conditions that faced Obama as he stepped into office. This background is important in order to set the proper context of President Obama's economic record.

President Obama had the following planks in his economic platform when he ran for President in 2008:

1. Tax relief-for middle- and lower-income Americans
2. Wealthy Americans would get tax increases
3. Technology innovation through clean energy
4. Prevent predatory credit card practices and reform bankruptcy Laws
5. Crack down on mortgage fraud
6. Protect homeownership
7. protect labor; i.e. union members
8. Promote free trade.
9. Reform Health Care

---

7 http://historyinpieces.com/research/us-unemployment-rates-president
8 https://en.wikipedia.org/wiki/Presidency_of_Jimmy_Carter#cite_note-.2770s_292-68

10.   As he took office, he also vowed to pass health care reform, and sign into law the Dodd-Frank bill.

After eight years, this is what he had gotten done within those economic planks:

1) Tax Relief:

- Expanded the Earned Income Tax Credit and Child Tax Credit for low-income workers. The Tax Relief and Job Creation Act increased the EITC through the 2012 tax years.
- Reduce self-employment tax. Done temporarily as part of 2010 tax cuts.

2) Technology, Innovation, and Creating Jobs:

- Tried to implement a cap-and-trade program to reduce carbon emissions by 80 percent below 1990 levels by 2050. Congress blocked it, but the number of coal industry jobs lost has topped 50,000. A record number of coal companies are also going into bankruptcy.
- Invest $150 billion over ten years to deploy clean technologies. The Department of Energy's strategy for FY 2014 was to double renewable energy production by 2020.
- Reduce oil consumption by 10 million barrels of oil by 2030, by doubling fuel economy standards within 18 years. The DOE's goal is to cut oil consumption by 2 million barrels per day by 2025.
- Make all new buildings carbon-neutral, or produce zero emissions, by 2030. Improve new building efficiency by 50 percent and existing building efficiency by 25 percent in

ten years. The DOE's goal is to cut oil imports in half by 2020 and double energy productivity by 2030.

• Eliminate special-interest business deductions, such as for the oil and gas industry.

• Double federal funding for basic research.

• Raise the minimum wage and index it to inflation. Obama proposed raising the minimum wage to $9.00 an hour in his 2013 SOTU, but legislation has not been passed.

3) Address Predatory Credit Card Practices and Reform Bankruptcy Laws:

• Establish a credit card rating system to educate consumers on risk. Create a Credit Card Bill of Rights to protect consumers from unfair practices, such as interest charges on fees and unilateral changes. Obama fulfilled these two promises with the Consumer Financial Protection Bureau.

4) Protect Homeownership and

5) Crack Down on Mortgage Fraud:

• Created a fund to help homeowners in foreclosure to either refinance or sell their home. Fulfilled through Making Home Affordable Act.

6) Work / Family Balance:

• Double funding for after-school programs. Obama created the 21st Century After School Program, which extends the school day itself.

- Expand the Family Medical Leave Act. Obama expanded it to flight attendants, crewmembers, and military families.

- Provide low-income families with a refundable tax credit to help with their child-care expenses.

- Encourage flexible work schedules. Obama has verbally supported it.

7) Protect Labor and
8) Promote Free Trade:

- More actively enforce and provide better labor protection for trade agreements. He hasn't fulfilled his promised to update NAFTA. However, he has included better labor protection in trade agreements he has signed with Colombia, South Korea, and Panama.

9) Reform Health Care

- Passed the Affordable Care Act.

10) Signed into Law the Dodd-Frank Law.

The interesting thing about looking at that list after eight years of a Presidency is—how many of those items above do not have any direct impact on the economy and jobs. So, what happened?

OBAMA'S ECONOMY

President Obama's approach to the economy is one that is a tried-and-true progressive view of the world. To pump the economic engine, he would use government stimulus—taxpayer funds—to invest in the economy. To pay for it, he would raise the taxes of the rich and wealthy; whom he felt had not paid their fair share. Investments in the economy would be in "shovel-ready" jobs within the infrastructure of the country. The mantra on this point was, "we are going to fix our roads and bridges." Clean energy technology would be the bridge to new higher-paying jobs and shift America away from coal and foreign oil dependence. Lastly, he would invest in the future of America by investing more in education. Those were the promises, but the question that matters is two-fold. How many promises did he keep, and what was the net effect?

The first step President Obama took was to implement a massive stimulus-spending package. Dubbed the American Recovery and Reinvestment Act (ARRA), the bill totaled 830 billion dollars. This money would be spent on clean energy projects, shovel-ready building projects, and tax relief to middle-class Americans. This last point was a major sticking point. Obama had campaigned against the Bush tax cuts, saying they were unfair. He even went so far as to make the argument that getting rid of the Bush tax cuts would help pay for the healthcare reform he wanted.

The only problem was that the Bush tax cuts had cut the marginal rate for all Americans. Middle class Americans were already paying a lower amount. President Obama was not proposing a further cut in marginal tax rates. But, he did say he would make sure that the majority of Americans got a tax cut. He did this in two ways. First, he lowered the amount of FICA taxes taken out of your paycheck. FICA is the money that gets taken out of your check on payday for Social Security and Medicare. By reducing the amount taken out, you have more money in your paycheck. The Obama administration claims the cut added 1,000 dollars per year back to Americans. Because most people in the country work for someone else, he could claim that he gave most a tax cut; even if the net result was only thirty-eight dollars ($1,000 divided by twenty-six pay periods) more in your paycheck.

But there was a problem. Social Security is a pay-as-you-go program, meaning that the money taken out of each check today is used immediately for current social security recipients. Take less money in, and you are shorting the program. The excess must be made up somewhere. That excess came from the business owners, i.e. the employers, of Americans. The amount taken out of an employee's paycheck may have been less, but the total, in general, did not go down. The government passed it on to the businesses and corporations that employ everyone.

The second thing that President Obama did was send a stimulus bill check to people. The average check was for two-hundred-fifty dollars. The checks amounted to thirteen billion dollars in payouts, and this payout was an awesome talking point. The President could say he was putting real money back into American pockets. Unfortunately, not all Americans got that money. It went to people receiving social security, disability, and disabled veterans—important groups of people who could always use more money in their pockets. Nonetheless, that is a far cry from "all" Americans. Most Americans did not get a check; which is good, since the government was borrowing to send the checks anyway.

The stimulus bill also put into place 224 billion dollars toward extending unemployment benefits. Under this program, someone who was unemployed could extend their benefit period from twenty-six weeks to as long as ninety-nine weeks. This would eventually provide a major smoke screen in evaluating the Obama economic era.

Let us pause for a moment and move to the subject of philosophy. Each party has one—a few actually. When it comes to Democrats, one of their core philosophies is that intention is what matters. They may not articulate it in that way, but it shines through in everything they do. You create welfare because you want to help people who need it the most. You want to lower obesity in kids and teenagers, so you make school cafeterias serve only healthy foods. You want to do good, and you evaluate yourself and others from that frame of reference—the intention to do good. However, once the good deed is done, Democrats do not stop and look at the results of their intentions. In life, it is not whether you intended to do good. It is whether you actually did well. Are you getting the desired result?

In the case of extending unemployment, you have the intention of making life easier for people who are out of work. A job search in a recession may take longer than anyone wants, and so extending the time frame to receive benefits is what you do. It is the compassionate thing to do. That is the belief.

And as long as people use it in that manner, you are fine and dandy. Except, people did not use the program in that manner. What happened instead is that people refused jobs that were either not in the industry they were used to, or if the pay was not more than their unemployment check, they passed on the job. They just kept taking the benefits, and eventually many stopped looking all together. How do we know this to be true?

The peak of unemployment during Obama's term was 10.5 percent. As he left office in January 2017, the unemployment rate was 4.9 percent. That is way down; which is a good thing, right? It means that more people are working now than when he got into office...

Except that's not what the unemployment rate means, and that's not the reality on the ground.

The government calculates the unemployment rate based on the number of people making claims for unemployment benefits. When more people make a claim, the unemployment rate goes up. When fewer people make a claim, then the rate goes down. This is a basic explanation, and at times can include other factors like Census surveys. But the measure is incomplete. There are groups of people not included in calculating the unemployment rate.

If you have exhausted your benefits, then you are not counted. If you are self-employed, you are not counted. If you are only working part-time, you are not counted. If you are not working, you are not counted. It is this last part that matters. If you have given up looking, then you are not participating in the labor market. Americans not participating in the labor market are not part of the unemployment measure, even though they are not employed. The government uses a different stat for this category.

The labor participation rate is how the government measures the number of people who are actually working each month. If you want to know how many people are working or not working, this rate is one that you must consider. In the Obama years, it is a measure that has been ignored. Interestingly, it is also a stat that shows the lowest labor participation rate than for any other President. See the chart below[9]

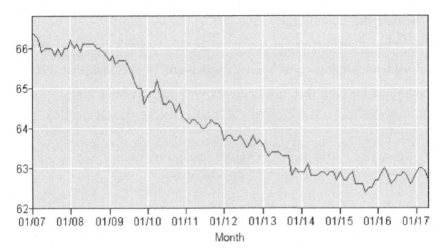

Notice how the chart moves further down as the years of the Obama administration are in office?

How can that be? How can the unemployment rate go down and the number of people participating and working in the job market also go down? It is simple; one measures people asking for unemployment benefits, the other measures number of people working. Think of it like this, if you send out invitations for your child's birthday party and ask people to RSVP; the number of people saying they will come is the unemployment rate. The number of people who show up for the party is your labor participation rate.

Per the Bureau of Labor Statistics, the real unemployment rate shows when the labor participation rate is considered is 9.5 percent. That is double the unemployment rate that is bandied about in the press. For those who doubt this number, it can be found when you go to the BLS website and click on "subjects," then "national

---

9 https://data.bls.gov/timeseries/LNS11300000

unemployment rate," then "top picks labor force statistics," and then "data tools."

The number of people working has not increased. What about the American economy?

The average annualized growth of America's GDP under President Obama has been 1.9 percent[10]. The national GDP numbers have, in fact, not been above 3 percent since 2005.

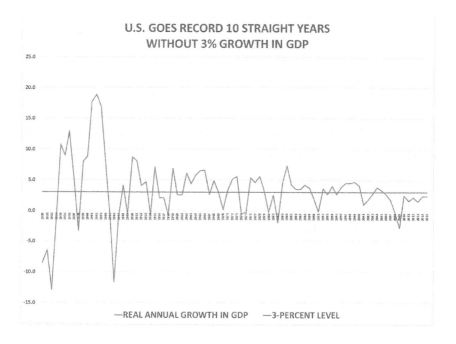

U.S. GOES RECORD 10 STRAIGHT YEARS WITHOUT 3% GROWTH IN GDP

—REAL ANNUAL GROWTH IN GDP   —3-PERCENT LEVEL

As the summer quarter was ending in 2016, the American economy had a growth rate of 0.9 percent. That is worse than anemic, but how does it stack up against former Presidents? President Reagan achieved an average GDP of 3.5 percent. President Bush after him 3.0 percent. Bill Clinton reached 3.88 percent. George

10 https://www.bea.gov/national/index.htm#gdp

W quietly got the GDP to 3.4 percent—just before the mortgage meltdown. When those last three months of his term is factored in, it drops to 1.6 percent. That is horrible to defend in a debate. This is not a debate, however. It is a book where I have room and space to point out the obvious. The average rate of growth in the economy under George W for seven years and nine months was 3.4 percent. Lastly, look at Jimmy Carter. Carter is soundly considered a failure as President, but even he eked out a 3.3 percent GDP growth. Essentially, every President in my lifetime has had better growth than President Obama.

There is something that is a bit more important than the average rate of growth over the length of a term: beginnings and endings. The economy has a habit of dipping—going into recession—during Presidential elections. The question is usually not whether the economy is in recession, but how bad. A new President is charged with getting the country out of recession, and doing so as quickly as possible. The beginning of President Obama's term started with a horrific recession. The greatest since the 1920's, for anyone who wants to listen. Unfortunately, a good speech line is not the same as reality. Yes, it was bad, that cannot be denied. But President Obama was hardly in a special place. Presidents Reagan, Bush, Clinton, and Bush all took over with recessions on their Presidential plates. The most comparable to Obama's would be Reagan's and George W's.

As each of these men took over the country, how well did the economy do immediately following the implementation of each one's economic plans? When Reagan took over and implemented the massive tax reforms, the US GDP grew to 9.69 percent (1981), dipped to 3.79 (1982) the following year, and then jumped to

11.39 percent (1983)[11]. The lowest it went under Reagan was 3.7 percent. When George H. Bush took over, the growth rate fell to 4.86 percent (1989), and then to 4.25 percent the year after. Clinton rode a wave of recession, and imagined collapse (GDP was at a rate of 6.66 percent growth Bush's last year in office... perhaps the number was a sign), but instituted a liberal economic plan in his first two years in office. The GDP fell to 5.00 percent. A new Congress came in behind Newt Gingrich, whom Clinton worked with despite their personal animus. A more moderate economic package was implemented, and GDP rose back up to 6.31 percent. The nation's GDP numbers remained in the 6 percent range for the balance of his term.

George W. Bush's term started with a double whammy. He took over after former Fed Chief Alan Greenspan had decided to pop the internet bubble via fed policy. A slew of companies with high stock prices, but no profits and little revenue did not help the situation. The market tumbled, and the country went into recession. Eight months after being sworn in September 11th, 2001 arrived. The combination left an aftermath of no growth. American GDP plummeted to 2.19 percent. Bush pushed a new agenda aggressively on both the economic and defense front. After his policies had got implemented, GDP rose to 3.76 percent (2002) and 6.42 percent (2003).

In the eight years that President Obama has been in office, the peak of US GDP has been 2.9 percent. That is the peak. That means the high point. To put this in stark contrast, when Reagan left office, there was a balance of 15 million more Americans employed

---

11 Source: U.S. Bureau of Economic Analysis

than when he took office. At the time I'm typing this paragraph, Jan 2017, the balance for Obama is 11 million.[12]

For anyone who follows the news or politics closely, you will notice the numbers are different from what are often cited for both Presidents. The difference is that these numbers are from non-farm payroll numbers. They do not include self-employment numbers, because self-employment is not, by definition, an employer/employee situation. But even if we want to throw the numbers the Obama administration likes to use, that would put Obama at 16 million jobs. The numbers bandied about between the press and Reagan acolytes is 20 million.

20 million is bigger than 16 million.

The numbers of jobs created is key, because while GDP growth is important as a measure of economic success or failure, it is a number that many do not understand. Jobs are easy to understand. Beside which, GDP numbers are averages. An average means higher in some places and lower in others. There are areas and groups within the country that have seen great growth under Obama. If you are in the financial industry, you have seen a record stock market run. The DOW sits poised to hit 20,000. If you are in the clean energy sector or solar industry, Solindra notwithstanding, the grants given out like candy under Obama's clean energy initiatives have been a boon. But what about the group to whom President Obama is most dear? How have African-Americans done under the first black President?

12 http://data.bls.gov/cgi-bin/dsrv

Kiara Ashanti

AFRICAN-AMERICANS
IN AN OBAMA ECONOMY

Shortly after Obama's win in 2008, a video surfaced of a young black woman saying, "I don't have to worry about paying my gas, I don't have to worry about paying my mortgage…" The clip went viral, especially in conservative circles. To conservatives, the comment exemplified the problem with liberals, a desire for someone else—the government—to pay their bills. I am sure the context of the statement was not that idea. More likely the woman meant that everything was going to be okay because everything would get better, not that Obama was going to pay her bills. Still, the emotion behind the statement does exemplify the emotions of the African-American community. The black community expected things to get better, and to get better especially for blacks. Yes, the President is supposed to be the President for everyone, but that is a general principle, one that is easy to say when every President before Obama was not part of a "group." And yes, to the people who think in such terms, white guys do not count. If someone from your group is in charge, you may want things to get better in general, but you want things to get better for your group most of all. Otherwise, what is the point?

While I do not subscribe to that view of the world, I do understand it. Take Nelson Mandela, for example. After years of imprisonment, he was released and entered negotiations with then-President De Klerk to end apartheid. If the end of apartheid had not come about after his release, what would have been the point? If it had crept back into existence after Mandela became President, what would have been the point of Mandela being President *to the black South Africans?*

Commander-in-Failure

The same principle was in play for President Obama. When blacks say the words, "my President," they do not mean because they are both American. So how did *their President* do?

For Obama's entire Presidency, the unemployment rate for blacks has been double the national average. When it was 10 percent, it was 22 percent for blacks. As he exits the Oval Office, the unemployment rate nationally is 4.8, for blacks, it is 8.8 percent.[13] Buried in the averages is a more disturbing stat. For American youth, ages 19 to 24, the unemployment rate for whites is 9.9 percent, while it is 20.6 percent for blacks.

The median amount of wealth for blacks has fallen from an average of $19,000 in 2007 to $11,000 in 2013.[14] Income, on the other hand, has only dropped from an average of $35,954 to 35,398—down 1.5 percent. All things considered, that is a bright spot.

In the 2012 Presidential primaries, candidate Newt Gingrich called President Obama "The Food Stamp President." The reaction to such a statement from a white southern politician was swift and predictable. It was roundly decried as a racist statement. Putting aside the assumption that the statement was about blacks, when more whites are on food stamps, is itself racist, then what is the truth behind the statement? As of 2013, the number of people on food stamp assistance rose to 47.8 million people—a 70 percent rise since 2008. In 2008 7.3 million blacks were receiving food stamps. Per the US Department of Agriculture, that number rose to 11.7 million in the same time period.

13 https://www.bls.gov/home.htm
14 https://www.brookings.edu/blog/social-mobility-mem-os/2015/01/15/five-bleak-facts-on-black-opportunity/

So thus far, we have less wealth, higher unemployment, and more blacks on food stamps… but let us continue.

Home ownership for blacks has dropped during his time as President. Not surprising given the housing market. Homeownership is down across the board, but he did sign the Dodd-Frank law and created a program to help homeowners in foreclosure refinance; neither appears to have helped the housing market.

Whenever there is an economic downturn, one area that has an uptick is the number of people going back to school. It's a way to improve your skills, gain new ones to move into a different industry, or just escape a bad job market, while bettering yourself. This is easy when you are young, single, and have no kids. If you are older, have kids, and more financial responsibilities, going back to school is a challenge. This challenge is magnified for blacks and Hispanics. Blacks as a group have the highest degree of households headed by a single parent—usually a woman. One parent means babysitting problems, a problem they face as working adults. But, when you add in additional hours that need to be dedicated to going to school, the difficulty is multiplied. Traditional colleges and universities are not designed for the life needs of working adults and parents. Even today, the number of evening and online programs from the traditional universities is small.

For-profit universities like DeVry, ITT Technical, and others, offer an alternative direction for working adults. They are designed around the needs of people who work fulltime or do not have the traditional background college and universities want. You don't need an SAT score to get in. This is valuable, because there are millions of black Americans that want to go back to school, but cannot get a quote "normal" university. They have GEDs, not diplomas. They cannot take a class at 10am and 2pm. In addition, many of the programs offered by for-profit schools are types that lead directly to jobs.

Anyone who has been to a traditional college knows that half the classes you take are useless for whatever given major you decide to take. Many of the programs available at a for-profit school are the kinds that focus on getting into the work place sooner. They are trades, like Barbering, Radiology, or electronics programs. They also offer many of the nursing and RN programs in the country.

But for-profit schools have been a target of the Obama administration. Regulators have gone after them for so-called predatory practices. They have attacked them on the idea of how many graduates get jobs after they graduate. They accused one school of improprieties, but never took them to court. They just withheld Title 9 funds for 90 days, which effectively shut the school down. All the students in the middle of their schooling were out in the cold.

The general beef with for-profit schools is the "for-profit" part. The general feeling of the Obama administration, education secretary Arne Duncan, and most Democrat lawmakers was that for-profit universities were more focused on making money than the students. In other words, they are for profit, but not for education.

This is an interesting tack to take, when traditional universities are more concerned with publications and research dollars. Otherwise known as profit by another name—without worrying about paying taxes, I might add.

Like any industry—especially one dependent on government dollars—there are certainly schools that did not do the right things. When that happens, it is the government's job to investigate, stop it, and curtail it from happening in the future. The problem with the approach under Obama was that they held the schools up to standards to which they did not hold traditional schools. Really, how many graduates of, say, Duke University, get jobs within three months of graduation? And they did not look at the effect it would have on the people going to the schools.

Many blacks and Hispanics go to these types of schools. The graduation rate for them is higher than for blacks of similar backgrounds who attempt to go to a traditional University or college. Going after these schools may have looked good in the media, but it had a negative effect on Obama's community.

On the primary education level, one of President Obama's first acts as President was to kill future funding for DC's Opportunity Scholarships. The move left 1774 black children unable to attend their chosen charter schools. Their parents had to find the money elsewhere, or send their kids back to the failing schools they were trying to escape. DC is a small area, but the move showed a larger theme. Charter schools and school choice were not on the agenda.

Obama increased funding for after school programs, but that funding was to extend the school day. It presumably was meant as an alternative means of childcare for working parents. But who wants to stay any longer in a school that is failing? The elementary, middle, and high schools are not directly connected to the economy. However, I placed this information here for one reason. If you cannot pay for a charter school, as a parent your first instinct will be to find the money. Usually, that entails a second or third job or a loan. All of these have negative impacts on a family's financial life.

Also affecting the economic prospects of African-Americans was the Obamacare law. As discussed, the law was supposed to give more people healthcare—and make it affordable. 21 million more Americans are reported to have healthcare now than when Obama took office. Of that total, a Department of Health and Human

58

Services report says only 2.6 million of them were black. Put in another way, only two million more blacks have health insurance than before Obamacare.

I have no doubt that the two million are grateful to have the coverage, especially if they had pre-existing conditions. But as discussed in the last chapter, that was not the goal. The goal was a whole lot more people covered and at cheaper rates. So what went wrong?

It is rather simple when you look at the demographics. African-Americans on the lowest economic ladder are also not college graduates, or trade school graduates. They are unskilled workers, with employment at places like restaurants, call centers, retail positions, etc. Many of these employers decided—rightly or wrongly—they could not afford the added insurance costs of mandated employer insurance. So, they cut their employees' hours to less than thirty each per week. Many blacks who had fulltime employment now did not. They were essentially turned into part-time workers. To be sure, this happened to everyone; it is not color- or group-specific. Nonetheless, it had a disproportionate effect on blacks, because of the type of jobs many in the black community have. Fewer hours means less income. Less income means that even if you get a subsidy for Obamacare coverage, you cannot afford the deductibles.

When the law was first passed, there was a hope that some people would be able to offset the high deductibles through a Health Savings Account (HSA). However, not all the Obamacare plans were HSA-compatible. Worse, the finalized regulatory rules essentially disallowed any HSA plans with Obamacare[15]. The new rules stated:

---

15 https://www.forbes.com/sites/gracemarieturner/2016/04/21/ health-savings-accounts-under-attack-in-obamacare-exchanges

1. The specified deductibles for the plans and out-of-pocket limits to be offered in the exchanges will be outside the requirements for HSA-qualifying plans.

2. Plans must cover services below the deductible, which are not allowed under the legal definition of HSAs.

This is another example of how politics gets in the way of progress. The only reason to limit HSA use in such a way is because money placed into an HSA plan is tax deductible. Democrats in Congress only like tax deductions when they are using them. Everyone else... not so much. The end result is that another path that would make health care insurance a bit more affordable for the black community was closed off.

In fairness to President Obama, the black community has lagged economically in all Presidential administrations. There is a saying, "When America gets a cold, blacks catch the flu," the basic sentiment being blacks fare the worst when the country is going through a bad time. That is statistically a fact. Even in growing economic times, say under the Reagan or Clinton years, the economic stats for blacks were far behind whites. Nonetheless, rising tides lift everyone. The black unemployment rate may have been higher than for whites under Bill Clinton, but it was still lower than where it is now.

In order for the financial prospects of blacks to rise, the prospects for America have to rise. If the economy is not growing, it is not possible for the fortunes of the African-American community to grow either.

Two years into the Obama administration, I started doing an internet talk show, called Urban America. It was like any other public affairs show, except we focused on how larger events affected the black community. One of the guests we would have on was a community activist in the true sense of the term. He knew what was happening on the streets and in the homes of the community. He worked with the Urban League nationally and locally. What I remember most is he would always complain about the high unemployment rate for black teens under Obama. If you could view snapshots of just those conversations, you would think he could not stand President Obama.

Alas, snapshots are not life.

He never wavered in his support of the President. No matter how bad the economic results got—as reported by himself—he was steadfast. No matter how impassioned, loud, or exasperated I got with him, he never wavered in his support of the President or his policies.

That micro example is the macro within the black community. Blacks have stood by the Democrats and their policies at all levels: national, regional, state, and city for the last fifty years. The results from these policies are of little importance. The democrats are the chosen team, and no matter how many losses or losing seasons the team has, blacks remain loyal to them.

The economic situation for the black community was not getting better, and was in many spots it was getting worse. The numbers spoke for themselves, but still, I was the traitor for pointing this out. Whether it was on Urban America, in radio interviews, comments on articles I wrote, or just plain twitter, the consensus was not Obama is failing, it was thought that I was an Uncle Tom. I was not alone in this treatment. Tavis Smiley was the go-to person for political and social commentary for the syndicated Tom Joyner radio morning show. As soon as he challenged what Obama was doing as it pertained to the black community, he was fired.

Tavis Smiley is no conservative. Still, he was treated like a traitor. This is something that white Americans do not have to deal with—this idea that if you disagree with a democrat or are not one, you are betraying your race.

All my friends know I have a huge heart. I would do anything for them. They know I care about people. They see how I conduct myself in everyday life, and are proud to have me in their lives. They consider me a quality person. I'm also considered quite smart. They know that I read incessantly, and am a complete news junkie. So, you can understand that it can be very... infuriating... when the topic of politics comes up and they throw all that out the window. Suddenly, the person who spends more time on news than they do does not know anything, is uncaring, and does not give a damn about people who look like me in the mirror.

Really?

I am a pragmatic person. My general view on all matters is fixing the problem. I do not care who comes up with a solution. I just care whether it works or not. I did not vote for Obama, but that would not have kept me from giving him credit where it was due. I did not vote for Bill Clinton when he first ran for office—I went the Perot route—but when he ran for reelection, I did vote for him. I did so because he deserved to be reelected. He was getting positive results. Considering how his first two years were a disaster, it showed he was willing to make a turn when it was necessary.

Barack Obama has never been able to do that. For all the talk about the Republicans not being willing to compromise, it was the President who never invited them to a sit-down. President Obama and his aides were the ones who would arrogantly claim, "We won."

The implication being to 'shut up and do it our way.' It was the President, via Senate Majority Leader Harry Reid, who shut down any Republican amendments to bills.

I believe this is because Obama is a true politician. What that means is that he is concerned with the optics, not the result. Throwing nearly a trillion dollars at the economy looks like you are addressing the problem. Talking about what Obamacare is *going* to do is more important than what it *is* doing in real life. Look like you care by extending unemployment, but say reports of people giving up looking for work are just lies from Fox News.

This intractability is the direct result of having been a state-level legislator and not an executive. Obama is a highly intelligent man in terms of IQ. But he has no wisdom or judgment. He never could gain it. Being in charge develops those traits. They come from experience; they are not God-given.

The economy is as close as a President is to running a business. In business, your profits and losses tell you whether your products are doing well in the marketplace. Sales and returns give real time information about the popularity of your products. For a President, the numbers you are given from your own departments tell the tale. If you throw a trillion at the problem and the results you are getting are not robust, you cannot stick your head in the sand and say we need more time. You should admit what the numbers are telling you. The current plan is failing.

Stagnant GDP growth, real unemployment near 10 percent, incomes flat or falling, businesses hoarding cash and not expanding— these were the signposts President Obama was ignoring. They are the waystations that tell the tale of his eight years in office.

CHAPTER THREE

THE PIED PIPER
OF VICTIMIZATION

Barack Obama began living with his grandparents at the age of ten. This did not occur because of the death, incarceration, or even financial destitution of a parent. President Obama's mother was alive, healthy, and well. She just chose to be an absentee mother, living in Indonesia with her new husband.

The right or wrongness of this choice is for others to debate. I bring it up because the absence of a parent—who is alive—has a profound effect on any young child. It is hard. It is emotionally damaging. Young children cannot process the nuances of adult decision-making. Everything is more simple and straightforward for children.

Am I wanted or not? Am I loved, or not? Both questions rattle around in the psyche of a child when a parent disappears. I remember in my youth watching my best friend wail, "My mom doesn't want me," after his mother declared she was leaving him with his stepmother. Even now the memory of that hopeless look in his eyes, staring at me like I could do something to change it, punches me in the gut.

Commander-in-Failure

I do not know if President Obama reacted in some similar fashion, either in private or public, I just know it was not easy. It affects everyone without question. I also know there is another question that haunts children left in his circumstance.

Am I a burden?

It is a question children ask themselves often when they are being raised by grandparents or other relatives. For young Barack Obama, the underlying tensions were sharper. He was left with grandparents who were white, and had never been happy with the marriage of their daughter to Obama's father—a man who abandoned his child and their daughter, proving their conclusions about him correct. Now they were faced with raising that man's son.

It is at this point in the story that the stage for excuses to be used later in life is formed. A young black man from these life circumstances often makes poor decision after poor decision—decisions and choices that often land them in prison, or worse. Society will then look at his past and say, "no wonder he turned out bad, he had no father. His mother abandoned them. They did not have the opportunities to be loved and cherished, as children should be." That is how the story usually goes, but that was not the life of Barack Obama.

His grandparents raised him, loved him, and made sure he got a good education at a private school. After graduating high school, he attended Occidental College. Two years later, he transferred to Columbia College, Columbia University; a school consistently ranked one of the top ten universities in America.

There are no public records regarding how well Obama performed, and the specifics do not matter. The academics were good enough to get him into Harvard Law school, the best law

65

school in the country. No one gets in without a strong academic background, raw intellect, and ambition.

If the story had stopped there, it would be inspirational. Young black male, abandoned as a child, puts the hurt and pain behind him to become a Harvard Law graduate. The story, however, does not end there. Obama would parlay his community-organizing street cred into local Chicago and Illinois state politics to become a statewide senator. He would marry one wife, remain faithful, and father two kids. He would give the speech of a lifetime in 2004, catapulting him into the national psyche and a US Senate seat. He would defy all odds, money, and expectations to knock out the Clinton machine to become the first viable black Presidential candidate for the United States. He would go on to win that race, cement his place in history, and do so in historic fashion.

The reality of his life is rich in positivity and inspiration. A living testament to the changing morays in America and its possibilities for blacks. Raised and loved by white grandparents, excelled in academics, and then placed in the White House by millions of white Americans. On January 20th, 2009, he embodied all that anyone— even black children—could be and do in America.

Barack Obama could say work hard, get educated, dream big, and go for it all, and you could be anything—including President of the United States—with ironclad creditability.

Instead, he chose to give Americans a different message.

On April 16th, 2008 in the debate between future President Obama and Hilary Clinton, moderator Charlie Gibson posed a question to Barack Obama.

GIBSON: ***All right. You have, however, said you would favor an increase in the capital gains tax. As a matter of fact, you said*** *on CNBC, and I quote, "I certainly would not go above what existed under Bill Clinton," which was 28 percent. It's now 15 percent.* That's almost a doubling, if you went to 28 percent.

But actually, Bill Clinton, in 1997, signed legislation that dropped the capital gains tax to 20 percent.

OBAMA: **Right.**

GIBSON: **And George Bush has taken it down to 15 percent.**

OBAMA: **Right.**

GIBSON: **And in each instance, when the rate dropped, revenues from the tax increased; the government took in more money. And in the 1980s, when the tax** *was increased to 28 percent, the revenues went down.*

So why raise it at all, especially given the fact that 100 million people in this country own stock and would be affected?

OBAMA: **Well, Charlie, what I've said is that I would look at raising the capital gains tax for purposes of fairness.**

We saw an article today which showed that the top fifty hedge fund managers made twenty-nine billion dollars last year— twenty-nine billion dollars for fifty individuals. And part of what has happened is that those who are able to work the stock market and amass huge fortunes on capital gains are paying a lower tax rate than their secretaries. That's not fair.

And what I want is not oppressive taxation. I want businesses to thrive, and I want people to be rewarded for their success. But what I also want to make sure is that our tax system is fair and that we are able to finance health *care for Americans who currently don't have it and that we're able to invest in our infrastructure and invest in our schools.*

And you can't do that for free.

OBAMA: **And you can't take out a credit card from the Bank of China in the name of our children and our grandchildren, and then say that you're cutting taxes, which is essentially what John McCain has been** *talking about.*

And that is irresponsible. I believe in the principle that you pay as you go. And, you know, you don't propose tax cuts unless you are closing other tax breaks for individuals. And you don't increase spending, unless you're eliminating some spending or you're finding some new revenue. That's how we got an additional four trillion dollars' worth of debt under George Bush. That is helping to undermine our economy. And it's going to change when I'm President of the United States.

GIBSON: **But history shows that when you drop the capital gains tax, the revenues go up.**

OBAMA: **Well, that might happen, or it might not. It depends on what's happening on Wall Street and how business is going. I think the biggest problem that we've got on Wall Street right now is the fact that we have a housing crisis that this president has not been attentive to,** *and that took John McCain three tries before he got it right.*

And if we can stabilize that market, and we can get credit flowing again, then I think we'll see stocks do well. And once again, I think we can generate the revenue that we need to run this government and hopefully to pay down some of this debt.

That exchange was a window into the underlying thinking of Barack Obama—a gaping hole into which anyone looking could see his viewpoint toward success. It did not matter to him that lower tax rates lead to more revenue. In his view, since the rate was lower and some hedge fund trader, business owner, or CEO were making millions of dollars more than the average citizen, you needed to raise the rates for fairness.

But what is so unfair?

Why would the fact that someone makes more than someone else mean it is fair to charge them a higher percentage for anything, simply because of their bank account size? When you go to a Honda dealership, they don't charge a doctor more for a Civic than a janitor. The car is the same price. It is, in fact, illegal to charge someone more for the same car, just because of their income, ethnicity, sex, or color of their skin. Somehow when it comes to the issue of taxes, we believe that it is perfectly acceptable to charge a millionaire nearly 50 percent in taxes, even though their income has nothing to do with the people who make only $30,000 a year.

The information provided in Obama's answer does not stop there. He goes on to give the further reason for the higher tax rate.

"But what I also want to make sure is that our tax system is fair and that we can finance health care for Americans who currently don't have it and that we're able to invest in our infrastructure and invest in our schools,"

In other words, he wants the rich to pay more into the system so that he can take that money, and give it to others in the form of health care, and education.

Take from people who have, and give the funds to people who do not have, and call that fairness.

It is worth noting at this point that Obama showed a lack of economic understanding in his remarks. If you want the government to take in more money to spend on programs, then logic dictates that higher tax revenues provide that extra cash. Gibson pointed out that more tax revenue is gained with lower rates than when the rates are higher. So, that means a lower rate is not bad because you are gaining more of what you desire, more tax revenue. But Obama—and he is not alone in this view—did not care about what the end outcome was going to be.

But why? Why does that bother him?

I could go further into the subject of the difference between income tax versus capital gains taxes. I could explain in more detail how Obama does not understand economics or the concept of static analysis. I could list the tax revenues of the government under Presidents who cut taxes versus raised taxes, but none of that would answer the fundamental question.

In subsequent years as President and in his speeches, President Obama provided the answer to the question. On the campaign trail for reelection, one of Obama's favorite lines was the following:

"I believe that this country succeeds when everyone gets a fair shot, when everyone does their fair share, when everyone plays by the same rules."

The anger that would course through me whenever I heard these words is hard to describe. And it was not just the lines of speeches like that, or hearing him talking about the fairness of taking more from others to give to the less unfortunate, or even flippant remarks like "at some point, you have earned enough money."

I am under no illusion that Obama did not work hard, or study hard to get through Columbia, or Harvard Law School. I am quite aware that taking a job as a community organizer is waaaay below the type of job he could have gotten. It was a sacrifice he made because he had a longer-term political goal in mind. There is little doubt in my mind, given the period he grew up in, that he had to deal with racial issues and prejudice. But he made it. He got to the number one job in the world, and yet he goes around the country telling people that for you to make it, you have to take money from someone else.

Make no mistake, when you say that taxes on the most successful in society have to go up for others to have a fair share and a fair shot, you are saying that for you to be successful, you have to take from others. When you say everyone must pay their fair share of taxes, so that everyone else can have a fair shot, you are implying that the only way the less fortunate can succeed is if the government levels the playing field through taxation. The bottom line implication is that if tax rates remain low, working class cannot become middle-class, and the middle-class cannot become the affluent class.

How in the hell does an unprivileged black man in America become the President of the United States and give that kind of weak message to Americans?

Is a higher tax rate responsible for Obama getting into Columbia University? No! I suspect his grades and SAT scores had something to do with that.

Is a higher tax bill for the Forbes' richest 400 Americans responsible for Obama attending Harvard law school, becoming law review president, and graduating law school with honors? I think not. I suspect, though I could be wrong, that hard work, long study hours, and good grades are what allowed him to do that.

The stark reality in America is that success in life has more to do with the choices we each make in life. He chose to pursue education; without his law degree, there is little chance he would have ever become President. So, it seems to me that using the bully pulpit of the Oval Office to stress the importance of going to school and studying hard is a better message to give than a message based on class warfare.

President Obama and Michelle Obama were—and still are—in a unique position in America. They are the quintessential examples of what can be achieved with the right life choices. Michelle is from the 'hood, but did not make "in the 'hood" decisions. She did not drop out of high school, as upwards of 30 percent of Chicago teens do. She did not engage in drugs. She did not get pregnant as a teen. She went to college, and law school after that. She is an American success story. She should be a vocal example of what it takes to succeed.

What we get from them instead are examples of victimhood thinking. They want everyone to have a fair shot at success, but think you must take from others to give that to people. Michelle Obama infamously said, "For the first time in my adult life I am really proud of my country," during her husband's campaign, when it looked it looked like her husband would become President, not while it provided her better opportunity than in any other country[16]. And as soon as the country choose Donald Trump for President instead of Hillary Clinton, she declared, "We are feeling what not having not having hope feels like."

What the hell does that mean? Why would any President have an ultimate say in how your life is going to turn out? Presidents can affect the macro level of the country, but they have zero impact on the decisions you make every day. The decisions that determine your success or failure come from within, not the President, not

16 http://www.foxnews.com/story/2008/02/19/michelle-obama-takes-heat-for-saying-shersquos-lsquoproud-my-countryrsquo-for.html

Democrats, not high tax rates, not wealth redistribution, and yes, not from Republicans either.

I'm writing this paragraph on a sunny, 79-degree day in Florida. I could be out in my garden. I could be shooting arrows at the archery range. I could be at my goddaughter's house playing with her. I could be at the bar. I could be doing anything else other than inside writing these words for you. If I decided to do those other things, I would fail in my goal to write this evaluation of our former President. Would that be the fault of some hedge fund giant?

When you declare that the affairs of others are a direct impact on you in the negative, you are turning people into victims. When you talk about racism, classism, sexism, and the unfairness of people getting rich, we are telling people they are victims in life.

Why couldn't our former President talk about American exceptionalism and how all things are possible in America without the government? Why couldn't he go to the churches in black communities and talk about lowering out-of-wedlock birth rates to help ensure a better future for you and your community? Why couldn't President Obama talk about why the rich happened to be rich, which is that they took a shot in life and opened a business? Why leave that message to the Republicans to give?

How is at all helpful for Michelle Obama to give a speech saying concert halls and museums did not welcome non-whites the way they do whites. She went on to say, later in that speech, that thinking and knowing you are not welcome at places like this (museums) limits the horizons of far too many of our young people[17].

Did she consider that hearing the First Lady telling black kids they are not welcome at museums, could limit their thinking?

17 http://www.washingtontimes.com/news/2015/may/6/michelle-obama-says-black-kids-feel-unwelcome-in-m/

Perhaps a message about coming to a museum versus hanging out at a friend's house playing video games, or making Vine videos would be a more appropriate message. Perhaps a message about how when she was a kid, she felt unwelcome because of the period she was born into, but today no one thinks twice about any black person going to a museum. After all, does anyone really think the museum she was speaking at never has black visitors?

As an American, I want to hear a President talk about solving problems and the promise of America. I did not get that from President Obama. I heard a lot about how my health care needed to be funded by other people. I can find a lot of words about spreading the wealth, from those who created it, into my pockets in one form or another. I can find sentiments about how, without funding for universal pre-K, all of our kids are going to grow up stupid.

DOES RACE STILL MATTER?

As a black man in America, watching a black man giving the State of the Union speech, I want to hear words of encouragement to black kids in America. I want him to talk about what has changed in America. I wish for poetic words and soaring rhetoric about possibilities.

I want the black man to talk about how race is not a major factor in the lives of blacks today. That is, of course, a message contrary to what many democrat blacks think. As far as many are concerned, it is just as hard today as it was in 1950.

Really?

Well, let's look at this for a moment. Barack Obama, a black man, is President. How did that happen? Millions of white people put him into office. So does that mean white people still hate blacks? I would think not. Have you noticed how the number of interracial relationships has skyrocketed? But I digress.

I live in Florida, the sunshine state. Do you know why they call Florida the sunshine state? Because it is always sunny in Florida. Sunny and warm.

That is, of course, not true. The temperatures can drop to the thirties in Florida. If you live in Jacksonville or in the panhandle, you could wake up in the morning and see frost on the grass. But if you ask the average person walking down the street, "is Florida cold?" They will say no. The reason is obvious. It is because *most* of the time Florida is warm.

What does this have to do with anything? It is an analogy.

When my grandfather was my age, everything he wanted could be denied him because he was black. He was called Nigger or Negro on a regular basis. Housing, work, pay, everything revolved around his blackness. Black Only was a thing, and White Only often meant more than a bathroom or restaurant counter.

The last time a white person called me a nigger was on Twitter. A white liberal did not take kindly to me making up my own mind up about whether or not to be a Democrat or Republican. Before he wrote those words, I had not heard the word—from a white person—for thirty years. The only people who say the word regularly in my life are other black people.

I know there is this argument within the black community that we have taken the word and used it in our own way. Hearing the N-word, as it's called now, from one black person to another is not the same as when a white person says it. When I hear that, and I usually respond with, "what about the white kid who grew up in the hood and is black in all ways except skin color?"

There has never been a profession I wanted to be employed in that I was kept from doing by being black. I have not been followed around the stores of the malls, even when I had dreadlocks. I have never been stopped by police just because I was black. Does that mean I trust cops like a suburban white kid does? No. Do not be ridiculous. But I do not think all cops see me drive by them on the highway and say "Oh, a black man in a car, let's stop him."

I can hear some black saying, "Well that happens all the time."

I do not know how many blacks have cars in America, but I do know that police stops in America do not reach into the tens of millions like it would if cops stopped every black person driving a car.

My point is simple. The number-one problem I will have tomorrow when I get out of bed will not be because I'm black. If you are black and reading this book, your number-one problem tomorrow when you step out of bed will not be because you are black either. No. It will NOT.

It might be that you are in debt. It could be that you want more from life, but don't have a college education. It could be that you hate your job. It might be that your boss has jungle fever and hits on you all the time. It could be that your man is cheating, or your wife is cheating. It WILL NOT, however, be because you are black.

Racism exists in the same way extremely cold days exist in Florida. It happens, just not that often.

America does not need the ultimate proof of the change in America, President Barack Obama, acting like the Civil Rights fight was never won. I do not want to hear words out of his mouth that signal to young black boys that they cannot make it. I have no use for the sentiment that my success is dependent on whether or not Uncle Sam can manage to ram through another round of high taxation.

In President Obama's fifth State of the Union Address, the phrase "opportunity for all" was used fifteen times. He stressed that he wanted to build an economy that was designed to give an opportunity for all Americans.

"The America we want for our kids—a rising America where honest work is plentiful, and communities are strong; where prosperity is widely shared, and opportunity for all lets us go as far as our dreams and toil will take us— none of it is easy."

What could be wrong with wanting every American to have an opportunity? How does anyone argue against that concept? Here is the problem—the statement implies you do not have access to opportunity already.

I dare anyone reading these words right now to name a single profession or job that exists in America currently that people cannot get. Go ahead and try to name something—lawyer, or doctor? We have plenty of those; black ones, white ones, Spanish ones, gay ones, and females too. Business owners? We have plenty of those, in all manner of ethnicities and sexes. Surgeons? My friend's surgeon is a Muslim and female. I am pretty sure my eye doctor is gay.

If you are black, you can find a black example of any profession you could want to have. If you are a mother who wants to give your daughter role models of women, you can do so in each and every single category of job. Are you black and from the hood? Cool, your homegirl Michelle is from the hood—she happens to have a law degree, She also happens to be First Lady.

'Opportunity for all' already exists in America. What does not exist, however, is equal results for all. The CEO of a Fortune 500 company is going to make more than the janitor who is a high school dropout. The brain surgeon is going to make more than the registered nurse. The CPA is going to do better financially than the social worker, or the fast food restaurant worker.

President Obama—indeed all liberals—equates equal results with fairness and opportunity. He wants to even the economic scales by trying to engineer the same results for as much of the population as possible. To accomplish this, his prescription was to mandate a higher minimum wage, give people healthcare, get rid of loans that people willingly accepted to get an education, and a host of other goodies doled out by the federal government. And all we had to do to have all those things was tax the rich more. If we did not, if the Republicans stood in the way of that, then they were choosing tax breaks for the wealthy instead of opportunity for all.

Imagine, if you will, your children. They are bright, maybe even gifted. You have high hopes that they will get into a good college, perhaps even an Ivy League school. You and your spouse make sure your kids work hard and study hard. It pays off. Your kids have straight A's, but then you go to a parent-teacher conference. At the conference, an administrator tells you, "Your kids have done exceptionally well. They have earned 4.0s all around, but we have some kids who have not done as well as your children. They are not lucky enough to have parents like yourselves, engaged in their child's life and education. The results these kids have are too skewed from the results of your child. So, we are going to be taking a few points from the grade average of the best students, and passing them on to the lower-performing kids. That way, there is a fairer distribution of grades and results."

How would that go down?

I am quite sure there is not a parent alive in this country who would accept that. Make no mistake, when you hear any politician talking about raising tax rates on the rich, they are doing the same thing I just described. It is the same concept. The only difference is kids are sacred, and the money of a billionaire you do not know is not—unless you are the billionaire.

The inherent unfairness morally of taking more money from person to give to another is one thing. President Obama, however, always went the extra step of making sure the masses understood that unless we did, the opportunity would either shrink or disappear.

The job of a President is hard. He is responsible for so many things; defense, economic policy, international trade relations, preventing wars or deciding to engage in one, etc. But he is also a symbol. The President is supposed to be a shining example of American values and promise. The President is just a man, but in America's collective myth, he is supposed to be a symbol of our best self. Strong, charismatic, hopeful, and inspiring.

Barack Obama was charismatic. He was certainly hopeful that he could push America closer toward a social democracy resembling Europe. But the only inspiration he provided was inspiring fellow Americans to covet and resent the wealth and success of others.

CHAPTER FOUR

HOW POLITICS KILLED AN ICON

When people think of the presidency, they often think about what a President can do. Declare war, propose and sign new legislation into law, use the power of government administrative rules to pass new regulations, nominate judges, or influence foreign leaders. These are the actions an American President oversees. They are what makes him the single most powerful man in the world. There is more, however, to the job than policy or a President's practical power. Image counts as much as substance. The President carries a large amount of gravitas—gravitas that can influence how people see the country, themselves, and the country's future.

This is one reason Donald Trump had such a hard time in the media. Americans want to look at our kids and point at the President as the ultimate shining example of what to be, how to act, and what it was possible to accomplish. Few felt they could do that with Donald Trump. Even if you liked him, I doubt you would tell your little boy to talk and act like him.

Obama, however, and his wife with him, exemplified that mythical Presidential image. They were shining examples anyone could point to and say, "Be like that." I'm not talking about policy here, or social values as they are expressed in political policy. I'm talking purely the image and attributes it takes to become the President.

There are numerous jobs you can get in America that do not require college. There are plenty of jobs that require a college degree, but do not require an elite education from an Ivy League school. There is one job that almost requires both.

The Presidency.

Since 1960, only three Presidents out of twelve have not attended an Ivy league school. President Johnson gets a mulligan, considering he became President due to the death of President Kennedy. If you want to be POTUS, then Ivy-league-bound you'd better be.

So, what's my point? It is simple. There is no better example of education's imperative than being President. If you want to be considered for the job, then you have no choice but to be a college graduate, and from an elite school. Americans consciously and unconsciously demand it. Sorry, but State U won't cut it.

Obama went to Harvard Law; so did his wife. In fact, Michelle is a double-Ivy-leaguer—Princeton for undergrad, Harvard for law school.

If you want to show a teenager how to do relationships, the Obamas fit the ideal. They married early, stayed together, and by all appearance, there is no cheating, and they have two kids. All they need is a slice of American apple pie.

What about how they carry themselves, apart from the politics. Can you argue against them? Do we doubt their love for each other? If you want to point to an example of partnership based on love or admiration of each other versus partnership based on ambition, who would you choose, the Obamas or the Clintons?

Kiara Ashanti

There are numerous attributes to the Obamas that make them inspiring figures. This matters, because they both carry a bully pulpit. The President's is obvious, of course. He is in the unique position of being able to get on television, radio, or into print any time he wants. He can highlight issues and problems at a moment's notice. If a President wants, he can effect change (or attempt to) in policy or national consciousness by simply using his bully pulpit.

The wife of a President shares this spotlight—especially in today's social media world. Eleanor Roosevelt was the first FLOTUS to understand this and use her unique position to highlight a pet project. Every FLOTUS since has had her own cause to champion. Barbara Bush worked on AIDS awareness. Nancy Reagan famously, or infamously depending on your point of view, started the "Just Say No" campaign against drugs. Laura Bush focused on literacy. They choose to do this because they understand that even though they have no political power in governing, they can be an influence in another form. First Ladies have their own spotlight they can use. They know it and know they *should* use it.

However, their choices of projects, especially in recent years, are not random. There is now a political element to the decision on what project a First Lady tackles. Hilary Clinton wanted to be involved with national policy as if she had been voted to a seat at the table. That turned out disastrous, and so she melted into the background. In response, Laura Bush went on a subject that may have been dear to her heart and important but nonetheless, could not engender controversy. Who can argue about the need for more literacy, right? More reading is a good thing.

Michelle Obama's educational and career background was similar to Hilary Clinton's, and so many wondered what she would do as FLOTUS. Would she stay in the background with a benign project, or try to be involved in policy?

I argue that the choice she was going to make, along with the choices her husband would make with his bully pulpit, would matter more than any other President. When you look at the Obamas, their backgrounds and political base put them in a unique spot. They are black. They are from unprivileged backgrounds. They hail from Chicago, a city beset with the cancers of gun violence, gangs, and drugs. In the case of Michelle's old neighborhoods, cultural pathologies feed generational dependency, lack of education, single parenthood, jail time, and a general lack of belief in possibilities.

President Obama worked in Southside, saw the challenges people living there faced firsthand, and witnessed the pathologies. Michelle grew up in Southside. She *grew up amid* the violence, drug problems, limited thinking, and social pathologies. The Obamas witnessed all the issues that Chicago and dozens of other inner cities across this great nation share.

They also knew how to escape all those things—Michelle, especially. Both were the in the unique position of being the most public examples *ever* of what is possible for blacks in America. The decisions and paths they each took that led to each other and the White House are lessons that should be highlighted, illuminated, and hammered home. The subject du jour for President Obama or Michelle whenever they would talk at schools, churches, or civil events should have been easy.

Getting an education. Finishing high school—without getting pregnant. Avoidance of drugs. Not joining a gang, or stopping gangs. Even talking about gun violence. All of them were natural, important issues for either of the Obamas, especially Michelle to tackle. They could speak to the issues in a way no other Presidential couple could do. The level of credibility both have on any of those issues is beyond reproach.

By default, they are both icons in American history and within the black community. Simply put, people would listen to them. In this arena, their words would carry a weight that could alter people's personal choices.

Do you think that is too much of a stretch?

Imagine this conversation or speech coming from Michelle:

"I understand that it is hard, y'all. I didn't just wake up and waltz into the White House. I've lived your life. I'm from the 'hood. But I got educated. I made sure I didn't quit school, engage in drugs, or even get pregnant. And I didn't do it because I thought I might be First Lady one day. I knew I wanted a better life, and education was the only way I could get it. It is the only way YOU can get it…"

Imagine a campaign for eight long years with those simple concepts at its heart. Are you really going to sit down with your cup of coffee and this book in your hand, and say, *"Nope? That would not have inspired even one person to change their lives."*

Name a First Lady who can say, *"I'm from the 'hood, like you."*

That is what we could have gotten; should have gotten. Instead, Michelle Obama decided to focus on reducing obesity in kids. When the project was announced, I did a double take. It did not make sense. It was out of left field. She had not worked on it before. There was little talk about obesity during their campaign. More importantly, there were better problems she could address—problems related heavily to African-Americans. Barack had to tow a fine line when it came to policies specifically for blacks, but Michelle had no such barrier.

Let's examine the choice Michelle made first.

THE LET'S MOVE CAMPAIGN

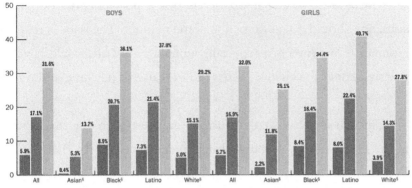

Obesity and Overweight Rates for Children Ages 2 to 19, NHANES by Gender and Race[11]

Note: The Centers for Disease Control and Prevention uses the term Hispanic in analysis. § = non-Hispanic.

Obesity in America is a problem. No one can argue against that. Adults and children weigh far more now than in the past. Per the

Centers for Disease Control, obesity in children ages 6-11 was seven percent in 1980. Today it is nineteen percent. It does not take a large leap of logic to realize that if the rates have nearly tripled for kids, then the news for adolescents and adults is not better. Thirty-five percent is the current percentage of adults classified as obese.

Obesity, especially earlier in life, causes several health issues: high blood pressure, diabetes, heart diseases, joint problems, and increased cancer rates for females. If you drill down into the obesity rates for race and ethnic groups, the news gets worse.

As the chart shows, in the race for who is more obese, Blacks and Hispanics are leading the way. Not exactly the type of race in which you want to be in the lead. Given the health ailments that can stem from obesity, and their medical costs, there is no doubt obesity rates deserve attention. It is a problem, and one with a high cost in dollars and lives.

The issue is not that obesity is not a problem. It's not that someone should not address it in some manner. The issue is that in a universe of problems, especially when a First Lady could have a positive effect for change, is *this* the best use of her time and bully pulpit?

Chicago is a city that is burning and has been for years. Not in the literal sense, of course, but it may as well be. In the year of President Obama's inauguration, 2009, there were 459 murders and 3,000 shootings[18]. As President Obama left office, that number had risen to 511 murders, and over 4300 shootings. The majority of the shootings and gun murders are the result of gang violence. Per the Chicago Crime Commission, there are over 600 gangs operating in the city of Chicago, with a total membership of 70,000.

Many of those gang members are uneducated boys and girls who did not graduate from high school. According to the Chicago Public School District, the high school graduation rate for black males was 66.7 percent[19]. That means 33 percent dropped out of high school.

What kind of job can a high school dropout with no skills get in America today?

The answer is, not a very good one. But a gang member can sell between 400 to 1,000 bags of heroin each day, netting $10,000. That's money you can live on. Of course, not every dropout joins a gang. Others get a basic job, making minimum wage, and rely on

18 www.city-data.com/crime/crime-Chicago-Illinois.html
19 http://chicagotonight.wttw.com/2016/09/05/cps-announces-re-cord-high-graduation-rate-class-2016

government assistance. A few go back to school for a GED, or go into the military, but not nearly enough.

Chicago is not unique in these problems. On a national basis, the graduation rate for blacks stands at 69 percent. Gangs, and the drugs they sell, are in all inner cities. Inner cities are rife with unemployment. Thus the money you make in the criminal realm is one reason so many join.

Another reason is the need for a protective family. Across this country, there is an epidemic of single women raising children on their own. Nowhere is this truer than in the inner cities of America and the black community. Sixty-seven percent of black children in the country are born out of wedlock. That is nearly SEVENTY PERCENT.

Making matters worse is that many of the parents became parents at a young age. They were emotionally immature kids, having kids. Many are reliving a cycle they witnessed themselves, as children growing up. Cycles that included abuse, social dysfunction, or just plain loneliness, as their parents were not around much because they had to work.

For people who align with a more progressive view of the world, talking about having kids outside of marriage in the negative smacks of old fogey-ness. We are in a new world, in a new time. People do not have to be married to love their kids. Marriage is one life option, not *the* life option to strive for in life. I understand the sentiment, even if I disagree with it.

Here is the thing. Single mothers in the 'hood, often have a "baby daddy" who is not taking care of his responsibilities. So, the mother is alone. That means one income, not two. That means along with the normal financial pressures involved in providing for a child; there are added expenses; daycare or sitters can mean the difference between being able to work or not. If the mother is limited in education, as so many young mothers are, then the job prospects are slim. Multiple jobs are often necessary. A second job means you are not there for your child. The emotional stress can make it difficult to connect with your child—assuming you have enough energy after working two jobs to try. When the kids are old enough to not need a sitter, then if you are not home, where are they?

I do not mean to paint a doom-and-gloom situation. There are certainly people who make it work. But studies show that two-parent households have better-educated, more evenly-balanced and well-adjusted kids. That is true because there is a stability… usually. It is also true that a two-parent home full of dysfunction or abuse is not good for the kids, either.

There are those within the black community who get offended whenever the out-of-wedlock rate within the black community is brought up. There is a feeling that it reinforces negative stereotypes about black people. Following up with statements about the social situation in inner cities usually leads to accusations of racism if you are a white person making the statements, and self-hatred if you are black.

It is important to note that: One, the descriptions are accurate for a large segment of people within inner cities who have had children out of wedlock, and Two, every single pathology mentioned above, and others, exists for the poor whites of the country as well. Go into the trailer parks of Tennessee, Detroit, Alabama, or anywhere else and you find the same issues. The difference—and it's an important one—is none of those trailer parks have the population density of Southside, South Central, Detroit, or South Philly.

And not for nothing, Michelle Obama is not from a trailer park.

Commander-in-Failure

Michelle did not land in her future by bouncing in from the affluent cul-de-sac suburbs. She is from Southside Chicago—the 'hood. She grew up in an area with dysfunction everywhere: social, educational, and economic. But she made it out. She is the ultimate example of the 'around the way girl who done good.' Great schools, excellent career, good man and marriage, and then First Lady of the United States.

She can speak to issues within the black community in a way few can, certainly better than any other First Lady. That should have been her priority. Instead, we got the "Let's Move" campaign. We were lectured on healthy school lunches, and regulations were even put into place that forced schools across the country to adhere to a set of mandated lunch items. Apples and broccoli in, soft drinks, cookies, and potato chips out.

Let's pretend for a moment. Let's pretend that after eight years, Michelle's pet project was so successful that child obesity rates went down to levels not seen since the 80s. What would we have in the black community specifically? How would Chicago look? The answer is we would have a boat load of skinny kids dropping out of school, joining gangs, taking drugs, getting pregnant or getting some girl pregnant, and the caskets of all the kids killed in gang violence could be smaller.

Yes, I am harsh. My last statement is purposely offensive. I want to make it clear. Obesity is a problem, but the problems of the inner city are bigger. If you change a person's weight, but their life circumstance is unchanged, then you have not helped them. A fat kid in college is better than a skinny kid in a gang.

I understand that some people might feel that I'm unfair. There are a million problems in the country. Is it fair to criticize Michelle Obama for picking a problem and not the problem *I* think she should have focused on? I get that, and there is a certain validity to the criticism. But here is the thing—I believe it is a matter of focus and degree of possible influence. The harsh truth is that the First Lady cannot solve either obesity or the issues in Chicago. Both situations are born in large part by a person's individual choices. High school kids across the country chose to ignore the new lunch standards, and tons of healthy food ended up in the scrap heap.

It is, however, about influence. What situation could Michelle Obama influence to the greatest degree? There is no doubt, none, that if the concentrated effort put into the Let's Move campaign had been channeled toward subjects of education, avoiding gangs, drugs, guns, etc., First Lady Obama could have done more good.

OBAMA'S LACK OF COURAGE AND CONVICTION

So, what does this have to do with President Obama? After all, the book is called Commander in Failure, not FLOTUS in Failure. The answer is that the choice of which Michelle's pet project is not random. Behind the scenes, there was a discussion about what to focus on. The political team of every President decides these things by committee. There is always a political component to the choice. I doubt the political operatives of the Obama White House focus-tested everything to the degree of the Clintons, but there was a discussion. Numerous choices were batted back and forth, each with different political implications and optics. No, I was not in the room, but make no mistake, this is how it is done.

Being black, from Chicago, and liberal put the Obamas in a bind. They are not stupid people. They are aware of all the issues

I have laid out here. Gangs and gun violence are not only obvious choices to attack, but as black liberals, it almost demands that they do. BUT—doing so had to be deemed too politically problematic.

It is the President himself who provides this proof.

The thing about a bully pulpit is that is revelatory. How you decide to use or not use it, can tell us a lot about the priorities, or mind set of the person behind it. The First Lady picks a single project. The President, however, is often forced to use it as events in the country dictate. A national story about a black professor being arrested for breaking into his own house will spur a speech about race and police. A mass shooting will spur a speech about guns.

An anecdotal story told by famed gun rights advocate John Lott illustrates all anyone needs to know about President Obama and guns. In his book, *On the Brink*, Lott recalls a time when both he and President Obama were guest lecturers at the University of Chicago Law school.

> *"The very first time I met him… I went up, I introduced myself, he said, "Oh, you're the gun guy," Lott said.*

> *"I said, 'well, I guess, so.' And he turned to me and said, 'I don't believe people should be able to own guns.'"*

There is little doubt that if—when asked—about the right to bear arms, he would say he supports the 2nd Amendment. That is what he would say. It is what all Democrats say, but nonetheless, it is a tenet of modern Liberal philosophy to oppose and to restrict that right as much as possible. Before he was President, he made no mistake about his dislike of guns. I do not think it would be a stretch to say he hates semi-automatic rifles. Lott, in his book, lays out four basic themes, as it relates to Obama's view on guns.

1. In a 1998 questionnaire for the Illinois state legislature, Obama said he wanted to "ban the sale or transfer of all sorts of semi-automatic weapons."

2. From 1998-2001, Obama was on the board of the Joyce Foundation, the "major funder for gun-control research" at that time.

3. Obama opposes concealed carry, and always has.

4. Obama only sees two "legitimate" purposes for guns: "hunting and target shooting." This means using guns for self-defense is not legitimate.

The last sentence is not one that I can confirm he has ever said, but given the other items, it is not too far of a leap. Obama's stance is clear. I know he does not like them. I know he has spoken out against them at times in the past.

Let me be clear. I do not support President Obama's view on guns. I have a right to own one, and the type I want. I am personally glad his view of guns is not the law of the land. I would never support the gun control laws he or Democrats want.

Nonetheless, in my view, Obama punked out on guns.

He wussed out on gangs and black-on-black crime.

President Barack Obama. The leader of the free world. Most powerful man in the world. Beloved icon of the media who can force conversations on any subject he wishes, at any time he wants. A man who married a woman from the streets of Chicago who worked in the neighborhoods and was their state senator for eight years.

In his time at the White House, his hometown political base saw 5,000 gun deaths and 12,000 shootings. The fuel for most of this violence is gangs. The people doing the shooting and getting killed are mostly black males. The most heart wrenching stories are always the collateral damage deaths the gang rivalries bring. Naturally, President Obama was speaking from the lawn of the White House every chance he could about this issue, right?

No. He was not. However, each time one of the fourteen highly publicized mass shootings occurred while Obama was President, he had something to say. In each case, he did the obligatory Presidential show of indignation and consoler-in-chief thing. Most of those speeches showed little anger and only small talk about guns. This only changed when a white Congresswoman, Gabby Giffords, was shot; a large number of white moviegoers were shot in Aurora, and after the shooting at Sandy Hook; when America heard him speak with anger, and gut wrenching emotion.

In total, over a 130 people died in the fourteen mass shootings under his tenure—basically one month in Chicago.

I do not believe that Barack Obama thinks of white Americans and black Americans in terms of which group is worth more. That would be an insult to him that I would not level. It is, however, odd that the President saved his anger and sadness for when large numbers of white Americans were gunned down. After Sandy Hook, there was a push for true gun control reform. Understandable, but couldn't he feel the same way about the streets of Chicago? He traveled the country after the shooting to try and do something about gun control. New gun control laws were out of the question, of course. A Republican-controlled House and Senate would not allow anything significant to be passed. I do not have a problem with that. So, what's my beef?

Easy. He should have been showing that same fire—always—when it came to what was going on in Chicago. *It's his home damned city*. Every weekend is a shootout. EVERY WEEKEND. Worse, Chicago—as bad as it is—is not even the worst city in the country for violence of this sort. Per a study by the Washington Post, Cleveland holds that unhappy distinction. Every week, there is an inner city that has multiple gun deaths. But, for the most part, President Obama was mum on it.

Supporters of the President will balk at this charge I'm making. Okay, fine. Can they show you and me the Blue-Ribbon group on gangs and guns? What is the working group that the President put together from day one on gang violence? How many speeches did a year he give on it? How many speeches did he give at black churches on it?

"Well, Kiara, the do-nothing Republicans would have stopped anything President Obama would have tried to do."

Who gives a damn what the Republicans would have done, tried to do, or complained about. Barack Obama was the President, not the Republicans. He was the leader, not Mitch McConnell. He is the President; *he* sets the agenda, not Congress, not the Senate. Last time I checked, the Republicans did not have control over Obama's mouth or speeches. He sure had no problem running his mouth about a "fair share," gay rights, or "George Bush's failed policies."

"Kiara, it sounds like you are saying you wanted Obama to do something about guns?"

No, I am not. I would have and did oppose nearly everything Democrats came up with after Sandy Hook. I like guns. I like them because they are one of my basic rights, and no one gets to tell me I cannot have one. What I'm saying is President Obama should have brought the issue out more often than on the tragic occasion of many white Americans getting killed.

I know that statement rankles many. I do not want to lose you at this point in the book. I believe All Lives Matter, without qualification. I get pissed when an innocent human of any color is attacked and loses their life. But I'm telling you, it is not a good look for the first black President to essentially ignore the death and violence that happens to blacks in cities across this country, *each and every week.*

It is uncomfortable to accept reality sometimes, but the reality is that for any other President, this pattern would have been just fine. It is not okay for the black guy. If we had a female President, and some city or cities were seeing 400 women killed each year in the streets, it would not be acceptable for the female President to not speak on it. Especially if she had a legitimate shot at effecting change in some fashion with just her words.

Barack and Michelle are different. Being the first in that position with their background means something. For many in the black community, it means everything. He had a responsibility to address guns, and more specifically the root cause of the violence, which is not guns, but gang violence. He had an obligation, and he did not fulfill it.

The only question is why?

OBAMA ON GANGS AND GUNS... IT'S COMPLICATED

Whether you are a person who believes in restricting gun rights or expanding them, either option promises a fight. The politics surrounding gun rights in America are one of three major political landmines, the others being Social Security and Medicare. President

Obama may have wanted a change in gun policy, but he wanted it in the abstract and did not want to truly fight for them. Let's be honest. He held the House and the Senate for two years—years he could have done any darned thing he wanted, but even he knew that gun legislation would have been off the table. If his name was Barry Smith, we could have just left it there.

But his name is Barack. He is black. That adds a layer of trickiness. There is no doubt gun violence affects blacks more than any other group. It is also true that if you start to talk about it, you cannot do so without dealing with who is pulling the triggers.

Black men in gangs.

Let me be more specific, because I'm a black man and I have never been in a gang. The people pulling the triggers are uneducated, poor black men, who feel there is no future for them. Based on their current circumstances, it is a legitimate belief. Bright futures are for those with education and skills. If you have neither, then your economic prospects in America—whether you are black or white—is dismal. Life in a gang, however, gives you a way to make money, lots of it. Being a gang member gets you street cred, a group of people who have your back; you even get some love from the neighborhood ladies.

If you are going to talk about gun violence in the inner cities in an honest manner, then you must talk about all of that. You cannot escape that conversation, and black leaders do not want to have that conversation. President Obama does not, did not, and for the foreseeable future will not talk about that. He will not go there.

This is something you, the person reading this book, should be able to understand. It does not matter what the subject matter is when something is wrong in our lives; we should look in the mirror first. The person staring back at us is the one most responsible for correcting the problem. The truism holds steady for groups of people as well. In politics and social policy, getting a group to see this is difficult. Most of the leaders of the group will say you are blaming the victim.

It is much easier, and in my opinion, profitable for the Jesse Jacksons of the world to blame the lack of jobs or economic opportunity for why the young men in the inner city move toward crime. It is much simpler to blame the NRA, gun manufacturers, or Republicans for the guns in the inner city. It is more politically profitable to bring the enduring American boogieman of racism to bear on why the inner cities are hotbeds of crime and economic failure.

If you are a white American reading this book, let me tell you what the average black person reading the last few paragraphs is calling me right now:

- Sell-out
- Uncle Tom
- Django (for Samuels Jackson's Character, not Jamie Foxx's)
- "Think you white."
- Coon

I could go on and on, believe me. I am called this because I have the temerity to look at my own people and call out the negatives. I point out the hypocrisy. I do not think Democratic values have helped our community.

If President Obama or Michelle had confronted these issues and the behaviors behind them, they certainly would not have been called the names I have been. Yet, the comment from Jesse Jackson in 2008, talking about how he would like to castrate Barack Obama when he felt Obama was "talking down to black people," demonstrated the high sensitivity to cultural tough love. I believe that if you could take the magical truth lasso of Wonder Woman, place it on Obama, he would admit going after the problems in the black community, caused by blacks in the community, would have left him open to criticism about blaming the victims.

That is one side of the issue. I also believe that in truth, Obama sees the behaviors that lead to drugs, gangs, and the violence that flows from them as the results of poor policy or a lack of money spent in the community. For example, if a young man has a good school and a job, he would not feel like he needed to join a gang, or pursue crime to feed himself or his family.

I cannot read his mind. My opinion on this is formed from hearing him talk about the lack of economic opportunity in inner city areas. It is colored by watching social justice activists get on television and immediately go there whenever someone brings up black-on-black crime or gangs.

I do know one thing. Every night, Barack Obama goes to bed next to a woman from the hood, and she made it out. I know that he is well aware that the vast majority of people in the hoods of America are not in gangs, even when they have the same social handicaps as the people who do join gangs. I know that his family is a testament to what is necessary for people to turn their lives around, or keep them from being turned around, to begin with. I know he knows all that, and I know he did not consistently use that history to bully-pulpit the issue as he should have. It is not enough for him to be the Commander-in-Chief and be seen walking around the White House holding his wife's hand. That's cute, but it doesn't nail any points home.

I know some could say I'm a little too optimistic on what effect he could have on these issues. A President has many issues to handle. Any number of groups and activists can yell about him not paying attention to their cause. I get that. I really do.

Here is the thing. Barack Obama was not a historical figure because of his views about climate change. He is not gay. He is not a practicing Muslim.

He is historic because he is black. He is historic because he did not come from extreme privilege. That's what makes him iconic. That is what gives him a certain moral authority, especially in the black community.

He wasted it, he and Michelle both, over politics. See, it does not matter if he would have succeeded or failed. Obama's background demanded he focus time on the issues of gangs and guns. The ultimate outcome did matter. A leader leads toward the desired outcome, regardless of whether they will reach it or not. The butt-hurt feelings of supporters or opponents do not matter.

In season two of the hit Netflix series, House of Cards, there is a scene of President Underwood, played by Kevin Spacey, having a meeting with congressional Democrat leaders. President Underwood is trying to convince the leadership to back an expensive jobs program. The leaders are hemming and hawing. Finally, Underwood has had enough. He tells them he knows all the problems, obstacles, and political risk, and then slams a chair against the table as he yells, "But I want you to fucking try!"

Obama had the high road, the background, the life example in himself and Michelle, and he did not even fucking try.

CHAPTER FIVE

RACISM USA

In 1619, the first captured slaves entered America. Over the next 245 years, America would be founded on the idea that "that all men are created equal, that they are endowed by their Creator with certain unalienable Rights..." built a country on the backs of people in bondage. It is the eternal emotional black mark in American history. It is the past that anyone can point to and say, "You did not build this country on your principles."

President Abraham Lincoln (R) brought slavery to an end in 1862. He fought a Civil War to secure that end. Blacks were free men, but despised. Slavery was not just about free labor. It was also about seeing humans as chattel; as "less than." This viewpoint, and the racist attitudes that flowed from it, would last 100-plus years.

It took a century to move the country legally into the realm where blacks could truly be considered free, as demanded under the Constitution. It would take at least another two decades for the vestiges of racism to disperse to the point that being black was not the number one problem an African-American woke up to in each morning.

At this point, many blacks would say that my last sentence has not yet happened. There is a contention that being black is still their biggest problem. There is a belief, held by many, that blacks are still universally hated.

As proof of that statement, we have a black man who became the President of a country wherein a scant forty years ago, he could only be a butler at the White House. Blacks represent twelve percent of the population; that's roughly thirty-seven million people in a country of three-hundred million. Twelve million blacks voted in 2008, compared to one-hundred-nine million whites. That means that Barack Obama became President because of white voters, not black ones. Millions of white people decided that a black guy with a funny, Arabic name that rhymes with Osama was better than a white war hero named John.

Let that sink in and marinate for a moment.

In a country that is still racist, according to many people, millions of white Americans flocked to the polls and voted for the black guy. Many did not just vote. They voted and cried when he won. They bounced around town with pep in their step, feeling more Patriotic and optimistic than they had felt in years. I remember the looks in the eyes of both white and black Americans. Blacks had a look of disbelief and joy at the historic moment. White Americans who voted for him had eyes that shone brightly with pride at America's accomplishment.

We had elected a black man as President of the United States, and most people loved him. The stink and stain of slavery and racism in America were finally washed away. America had reached a post-racial threshold.

Writing those words breaks my heart because that's not what we got.

The context in life is everything. Words, actions, even images take on a different meaning in isolation from their beginning and ending parts, and the events surrounding them. Throw in an individual's own internal biases, and you have a potent mix of toxic soup.

Ask the average black person about the treatment of President Obama during his term, and you will inevitably get "racist, nasty, and disrespectful." As far as blacks are concerned—heck, you can throw liberal whites in the mix as well, racism and bigotry were the fuel behind the "hatred" of Barack Obama.

Look at the current President Donald Trump, who spent years claiming that Obama was perhaps not an American citizen. Congressman Joe Morgan broke tradition and all proprietary shouting out, "You lie," twice during President Obama's State of the Union speech in 2009. Consider the vitriol of talk radio toward Obama. Or then-Minority leader of the Senate, Mitch McConnell, saying it was his job to make sure Obama failed.

Social media adds fuel to the fire. Twitter, Facebook, and Instagram are all mini-surveys on the state of how the American public feels about everything. The modern-day water cooler on steroids showcased the divide on Obama starkly. Opponents attacked him, and his supporters defended him. Meme after meme went viral mocking Obama; a few showcased him as a monkey. Conservatives routinely called him stupid, arrogant, a narcissist, a liar, un-American, and unqualified.

They said this about a black man who went to Columbia University and graduated from Harvard law school. A man who spoke eloquently, and with the appearance of considered thought. Clearly, there can only be one reason for this… despisement on the part of white Americans (this line is phrased this way purposely) for a black man. They cannot handle a black man being in charge.

America is a racist nation, and we see the proof in the treatment of our first black President.

If an alien species with an understanding of racial bias had shown up during the term of President Obama, perhaps they would have come to the same conclusion. He is black, and many whites opposed him on everything. How could one argue against it, right?

The answer to that question is context.

In 1998, President Bill Clinton was officially impeached for lying under oath about his relationship with Monica Lewinsky. This event occurred in the House of Representatives. The Senate did not reach the required two-thirds vote to fully carry out the impeachment and remove him from office. But the Republicans tried HARD.

Type in a Google search: "deaths under Bill Clinton" and you will get a cornucopia of results about the idea of the Clintons having people killed. The most famous of these deaths are Marc Rich, James McDougal, and Ron Brown. These are not just fringe groups. Rush Limbaugh, as widespread as any conservative, has talked about the belief and evidence that the Clintons targeted these people. As far as many are concerned, Bill Clinton is a murderer, and they have said it for years.

They have also called Bill Clinton a rapist. Kathleen Willey had accused Clinton of sexually assaulting her during his first terms as President when she was a White House volunteer aid. Paula Jones, Linda Tripp, and Gennifer Flowers have also accused him of sexual "misconduct" toward them. So, a large swath of Republicans considered Clinton a rapist and sexual predator (side note, yes I am aware of the irony here, after the hubbub over Trump's comments with Billy Bush) and proclaimed it loudly.

That's context number one. This is context number two.

President George Bush sent America into war after the 9/11 attacks. The reason—according to the Left—is he lied to get oil. He lied so he could have revenge on Saddam Hussein for ordering an assignation order on his father. He is also called a mass murderer, by the left. Keith Olbermann, former anchor at MSNBC, called President Bush "a fascist," "mass murderer," and "stupid" on more than one occasion. Former Speaker of the House Nancy Pelosi had this to say about President Bush:

> *"I believe that the President's leadership in the actions taken in Iraq demonstrate an incompetence in terms of knowledge, judgment, and experience in making the decisions that would have been necessary to truly accomplish the mission without the deaths to our troops and the cost to our taxpayers."*

Basically, Bush is incompetent, unknowledgeable, and lacks judgment.

Social media was still a pipe dream during most of Bush's term, and a nascent internet curiosity as he left office. But people did catch up. There are hundreds (thousands?) of memes depicting George Bush as a chimp—most famously as a mash-up of Alfred E. Neumann from Mad Magazine. The idea that Bush is unintelligent is not even a topic up for debate among Democrats. Their attitude, if you ask them about it, runs along the lines of, "I know you may like him, but of course, he is stupid."

On more than one occasion in this country and abroad, Bush has been burned in effigy… as has probably every president in recent history.

I could go on, but it is not necessary. The point should be clear. Former Presidents, all who are white, have been savaged in the media and by Americans before. The only difference between Clinton and Obama is that Obama is black.

Whenever this issue has come up in radio shows I have been a guest on, or in debates in the social media world, my message is simple. Barack Obama is not special.

Being the first black President of the United States makes you historical. It does not mean you are special. You are not immune to the fair, unfair, mean-spirited, or inane criticism. Obama does not get a pass on poor treatment just because he has a permanent tan.

Take the worst thing ever said about Obama, and it is still not impeachment-worthy. I'm going to repeat this. Bill Clinton was impeached. Republicans tried to, and damned near got him removed from office. Nothing even close to that happened to Obama.

No one has ever called Obama a rapist. Many call Bill Clinton a rapist to this day. Obama has been called stupid. So has President Bush, a man who went to Yale AND Harvard Business school. In fact, every single Republican President or nominee in my lifetime has been called unintelligent. Obama has been depicted as a monkey. So has President Bush. In fact, monkey photos in political cartoons of Bush were around long before Obama became a household name.

President Obama is NOT special. He is just black.

The hope of a post-racial America evaporated quickly after Obama's election win. Any opposition to Obama's agenda was coined as being racially motivated. If you did not want the country spending a trillion dollars in stimulus, you were a racist. Did not like Obamacare, racist. Made fun of his big ears, racist. If you reminded people that Obama had no executive experience and therefore was not qualified to be President, then guess what guys and gals, you were a racist.

This accusation started against conservatives, but soon shifted toward whites in general. As the fight regarding Obamacare heated up, it became clear in the polls and surveys that many of the people who voted for Obama did not like what he was doing. These people were called—you guessed it—racist.

Think about this for a minute. Look at the context in its fullness. "Whites did not like *President* Obama because he was black." Well, how the hell did he get the title? If every single black person voted for Obama, and all the black-hating whites voted for a guy named John or Mitt, Obama would have lost in a landslide. He was the first because people did not care that he was black. They liked what they heard from him. When the reality of what he was doing appeared, many changed their minds, and ended up being labeled as racist.

The history of America is one that makes the accusation of racism still a powerful tool. Call someone a racist, and they instantly go on the defensive. The primary subject of discussion or debate disappears the moment the charge is thrown out there, as the accused person will now try and convince you they are not racist. What lingers later, though, is worse.

Here is what happens. Let's say someone voted for Obama, but now has an issue with the concept of Obamacare. They turn on a news show or read Facebook conversations, and they see they are being called racist. They become indignant. They voted for the man, for God's sake. *"I am NOT racist,"* goes through their mind, and then a feeling of resentment begins to breed. A resentment against black leaders, liberal pundits, and anyone who would judge them in that way.

Race relations were supposed to get better under Obama. That was the assumption after he won the Presidency. However, a poll conducted by CNN shows the opposite. Fifty-four percent of

Americans feel race relations have gotten worse under President Obama[20].

There are those who will say that electing a black president did not mean the underbelly of racism in America no longer existed. A black President did not stop cops from shooting black men. Injustices in the social, economic, housing, and any other realm you can think of would still run rampant. A black president could not stop any of that. The general thought of liberal whites and blacks alike may be that having a black man as president to attack just exposed the lingering racism in the country.

In truth, what was exposed was not the racism of white Americans. Americans who do not like blacks have never hidden. The reality is, we are living in a different America than in the past. You do not see rampant racism in everyday life because most white Americans are not racist.

No, what was exposed was the racial chip many blacks carry on their shoulders. America is decades removed from the Democrat institution of Jim Crow laws, but millions of blacks act like it is still 1955. Every disagreement or slight is racially motivated. If you don't get the promotion at work, it is the white man holding you down. Cops do not overpolice or harass blacks because they are assholes, it's because they woke up with hatred in their hearts for black people. Hollywood did not nominate a black movie for an award because they are racist. Talking about the record increase in food stamps under President Obama is racial code. Black Lives Matter, but saying the life of someone else matters is racist. The prevailing belief in the black community is that in any area and in

_____

20 http://www.cnn.com/2016/10/05/politics/obama-race-rela-tions-poll/

every context, anything negative directed toward or about blacks is racist.

I see this point of view on Facebook daily. I see it in the words of pundits like Dr. Marc Lamont Hill, Eric Dyson, or Vann Jones. NY Times columnist Charles Blow never saw a subject he couldn't make about race. Sheila Jackson of the Atlanta Constitution and the Washington Post's Eugene Robinson appear to have a racism quota for their weekly articles. MSNBC loaded their evening line up with racial hucksters in the form of Al Sharpton, Melissa Harris-Perry, Touré, and Joy-Ann Reid. A white American cannot watch the news without hearing someone tell them they hate blacks; which is news to those who voted for Obama, date black people, or have black friends and coworkers they love. No matter what the subject or the issue for many blacks, especially those working in media, it is the fault of the white male boogie man. Self-reflection, i.e., looking at any other possibility, is summarily dismissed.

A snippet from my own life provides a great example of this in everyday life. Years ago, I worked as a financial advisor for Merrill Lynch. The market crash had not yet taken Lynch down, and so it was still one of the premier advisory firms in the world. I worked in a department that had 176 associates. I was one of five blacks working in the department.

Our jobs were as advisors and salesmen. We were paid a salary, plus a monthly bonus based on our production and new investment money brought into the firm. Best job I ever had.

A year into the position, I was called into the office of the floor manager. He wanted to know if I had felt uncomfortable. He asked if I felt anyone was treating me different from anyone else. The look I gave him was a clear answer. I did not and was confused as to what in the hell he was talking about. The other four blacks in the department were suing for discrimination. They felt they were not being given the same opportunities as everyone else. They had not been approached for promotions. Extra training opportunities were not being extended to them. They alleged that career growth and development could not happen for them as it supposedly had for all the white advisors on the floor.

It was all a bunch of blahooey.

Remember that word context? It was true none of the four blacks were offered promotions. Special training seminars at the home office that could lead to higher promotions were never extended to them. It is also true that at the time they made the racism charges, they did not have any hope for career advancement. That was because it was also true that they NEVER hit their monthly sales quota. The amount of new investment they brought into the firm was dismal. How do I know? Because some sales environments are still old school. You cannot hide your numbers, because everyone's numbers are posted, and ranked from the most to the least. They were always near the bottom.

I, however, was always in the top ten in sales. I always got current clients to transfer money from their other firms over to Lynch. I did not just meet the threshold; I always exceeded it. I was offered the role of team lead more than once. I was being considered for management. The sales director spoke to me about getting me into the higher training programs and seminars. My possible career advancement was just fine.

I was black. I had an African name. And oh yeah, I wore my hair in dreadlocks down to my shoulders.

I would think the difference would have been obvious. The others had not performed. I had exceeded the desired performance.

Thus, I was being offered the opportunities they were not. They were denied them because they flat-out did not deserve them.

My experience is not the experience of others. I am aware of that. I have no doubt that racism occurs in the workplace, and in general life. The point of my story, however, is that these fellow black Americans did not even look at what *they* were not doing. They shifted the blame onto racism instead.

The same phenomena occurred when Obama was President. Conservatives are known for hating high taxes and government spending; that is their platform, and has been for decades. But somehow when Obama started talking about raising taxes and started spending money like a drunken sailor, the conservative opposition was racist. The Tea Party started *under President Bush* and then gained steam under Obama with the push for Obamacare. Yet, the head of the NAACP, Ben Jealous, was running around calling the Tea Party remnants of the KKK, David Duke, and some Sisters of Confederate something-or-other that no one had ever heard about. They even accused them of calling members of the Congressional Black Caucus the N-word. Interestingly, when the late conservative provocateur Andrew Breitbart offered $100,000 for anyone who could provide proof, no one has ever offered to do so. In a world where there's a camera in every pocket, you are left with no choice but to assume the charge was a lie.

Is all this Barack Obama's fault? Yes. Yes, it is, because he never put a stop to this nonsense. It is his fault for always making comments about fear of the other, or "those who have antipathy toward those who look different than them."

There is no White House that ever does not know what is being said about it in the media. The staff and the President are always aware of what their opponents and supporters are saying. Did

Obama ever address this idea that every criticism or opposition to his agenda was always racist? Seldom.

In an interview with CNN's Fareed Zakaria near the end of his term, President Obama had this to say:

> *"Are there folks whose primary concern for me has been that I seem foreign—"the other"? Are those who champion the birther movement feeding off of bias?" Obama asked rhetorically. "Absolutely."*

> *"I think there's a reason attitudes about my presidency among whites in northern states are very different from whites in southern states."*

How can America move to a post-racial attitude if the President has views like this in his head?

Our black President failed to remind people that the only reason he was in the Oval Office and re-elected is because America has changed. One of his biggest supporters is a black woman named Oprah, loved and adored by millions of white Americans. We have had two black Secretary of States in this country. We have blacks loved and admired all over this country. Some are liberals like Oprah. Some are conservatives like Condi Rice or Dr. Ben Carson. Millions of people love them. Most of those people by sheer numbers are white.

I would get so frustrated about this aspect of the Obama years. It grew tiresome to hear legitimate concerns about the problems with Obamacare, or government spending reduced to a discussion about a white person hating the black guy. Guess what? Bill Clinton was white, and a Republican congress forced him to reduce taxes, cut spending, and engage in welfare reform. They fought with Bill tooth and nail. If the opposition is all about race, shouldn't the other old white dudes have just done what Bill wanted? President Carter was, until the 44th President, considered the worst President in modern times. He is lampooned always by the Right, but he is white, too. Maybe, Republicans just hate white, southern guys along with blacks?

In this age of photo apps, the creation and sharing of photo memes are as common as a phone call or handshake. Some are funny; others are offensive. Sometimes they hit the heart of truth dead center. I saw one recently that summed up the issue of race, as it pertains to Obama, perfectly. The meme was a split photograph; one side was President Obama, the other side President Trump. The words beneath the photos read:

"When whites opposed Barack Obama, they were called Racists. Blacks who oppose Donald Trump are called Activists..."

Of course, saying these things makes me a soldier for whites in the eyes of most black people. I am protecting my white masters. I always found the sentiment amusing. The very definition of social justice and Democratic policy is asking for someone else to give you something. You can bandy about whether you deserve it or not, but you are demanding something from someone else, rather than getting it on your own.

Myself and other black conservatives are mentally enslaved somehow, but black democrats are the ones saying they cannot have nice things. Is there anything in life more disempowering than believing that you cannot do something? That you have no control?

I found it to be a sad waste of intellect and resources. The talent that is in the black community is awesome to behold. Think about how the black culture has shaped American culture.

Music. Fashion. Speech and cultural slang. Sports. Those are the obvious things, but are the tip of the iceberg in what's possible. But it's all stuffed down under a mountain of racial angst and pain that 80 percent of blacks have never experienced. Vann Jones never went through Jim Crow. He is married to a white woman, for Christ's sake. Touré is married to a white woman as well. Both get to walk around without fear of getting shot for it. Try that in 1940s America.

The evidence of the new America is around us all every day. Yes, racists still exist. Yes, people, including blacks, still have their cultural bias. The question is to what degree it holds you back in life. Can it stop you?

There is a made-for-television movie about real life medical and surgical pioneer Vivian Thomas, a black man, and Dr. Alfred Blalock. Thomas was the brains behind the techniques for treating so-called blue babies. He was not a doctor. He had all the skills, all the intellect, but he was not allowed to become one because he was black. He was held from reaching his full potential because he was black. That DOES NOT HAPPEN to any black person today.

No one!

Here is the truth about America. The country is no longer a racist country. Period. There is no debate on this point, whatsoever. Are there *people* who are racists? Yes. In a country of 330 million, you will have racists, sexists, and people who think the earth is flat. You have people who believe in UFOs and that Bill Clinton sent black helicopters around the country to spy on you. The existence of one thing does not mean it is what you encounter every day. I've been around enough white people to know they really don't think about blacks that much. It is not a topic of conversation the way whites are in the black community. They are concerned about their kids, their family, their job. As the saying goes, "half the people are not thinking about you, and the other half don't care about you."

When President Carter was raising taxes and spending money, Republicans opposed him. Republicans do not like high taxes and spending. When Bill Clinton raised taxes and wanted to over spend, the Republicans opposed him. When they took the House and Senate, they forced him to lower spending and taxes in key areas. When President Obama came into office, he wanted to raise taxes and spend a lot of money. The Republicans opposed him, too.

Do you see a pattern here? I do. It's called Democrats like high taxes and spending, and Republicans oppose them. Carter, Clinton, and Obama, all Democrats. Each one wanted more spending and higher taxes, and Republicans fought them. Race had nothing to do with their decision. If Hillary had beaten Obama, they would have opposed her as well.

In 2008, Barack Hussein Obama electrified the country with uplifting rhetoric and a message of change. Change from the previous administration, change from the politics of the usual, change in the view of the country from the world outside of America. Americans bought into the message, and they could have cared less he was black. Hell, they loved that he *was* black. When the results of his change came back, people did not like it. That is not racism. That is simply buyer's remorse. He is not the first President it happened to, and he won't be the last. His race has zero to do with it.

CHAPTER SIX

AMERICA'S CHAMBERLAIN

The settlement of the Czechoslovakian problem, which has now been achieved, is, in my view, only the prelude to a larger settlement in which all Europe may find peace. This morning I had another talk with the German Chancellor, Herr Hitler, and here is the paper which bears his name upon it as well as mine. Some of you, perhaps, have already heard what it contains, but I would just like to read it to you: '... We regard the agreement signed last night and the Anglo-German Naval Agreement as symbolic of the desire of our two peoples never to go to war with one another again.

Later that day, outside 10 Downing Street, the following words concluded the assessment:

My good friends, for the second time in our history, a British Prime Minister has returned from Germany bringing peace with honour. I believe it is peace for our time. We thank you from the bottom of our hearts. Go home and get a nice quiet sleep.

The date was September 30, 1938. The speaker, British Prime Minister Neville Chamberlain. On that day, the Munich Pact was signed by Chamberlain, along with Adolf Hitler, Benito Mussolini, and French Premier Edouard Daladier, handing Czechoslovakia over to the Germans. The agreement was struck because that was the only way for peace to occur. If Chamberlain had refused, then the war would have come to Britain.

But he signed the accord, and as he said, "We can have peace in our time… Go home and get a nice quiet sleep."

Peace did not come. In two years' time, quiet sleep eluded British citizens as Germany began air raids against British cities. London was bombed seventy-one times. In all, over one-hundred tons of bombing ordnance was dropped on at least sixteen British cities. Still, England escaped the worst of it. Adolf Hitler sent the German army into the Netherlands, Belgium, Luxembourg, Denmark, Yugoslavia, Greece, Norway, Western Poland, and appropriately enough, France. They occupied all those countries, and but for the US, they would have taken parts of England, if not London as well.

History has a way of softening the view of some of the mistakes leaders make while in office, battle, or war. Excuses that were not tolerated at the time are given voice over time. In the case of Neville Chamberlain, the record is still mostly intact and justified. He is the living embodiment of the word *appeasement.*

The dictionary gives that word a definition of "a political policy of conceding to aggression from a warlike nation." It is spot-on if you are in the hallowed halls of a university, waxing poetic about history. In reality, appeasement is nothing more than the result of fear and naiveté—fear of fighting, and being naïve over your ability to reconcile with irreconcilable people.

Simply put, if you see a bully hit everyone around you, and he walks over to you, there are two choices. You either fight him, or you get hit. Trying to talk to the bully about why he should not hit you is deciding to get hit.

When Barack Obama came into office, he was not facing any invading countries. In his view, the invading country was the US The war in Iraq was still ongoing. The Afghanistan war was plugging along, albeit with fewer resources dedicated to it. The American public and many world leaders were bluntly sick of it. The war on terror was and is not like any other war. The terrorists are hiding and training in different Muslim countries, but the countries themselves are not fighting the US. At least, not out in the open. The view of America was declining. Perhaps the biggest examples of this are open protests, effigies of President Bush burning when traveling to Europe, and an Iraqi journalist throwing a shoe at him. Apart from the violence of the act, it is also seen as an ultimate sign of disrespect in their culture.

Obama's election elevated America's image abroad. The masses in the US were not the only people who loved him. Europeans fawned on him as well. This culminated in the ultimate demonstration of emotional feeling about Barack Obama; he won the Nobel Peace prize before doing a damned thing as President. The prize committee had this to say about their decision:

"For his extraordinary efforts to strengthen international diplomacy and cooperation between peoples."

Of course, he had not done anything yet, but the committee was hopeful and could tell he wanted cooperation, not war. This would become a hallmark of Obama's public persona. A man who was diplomatic, conciliatory, and reasonable. He was measured, not a cowboy like Bush.

Unfortunately, measured is not the correct word. Meek is a more apt description. Chamberlain-like would be the historical comparison. It is not a nice charge, but it is justified.

Obama started the road to appeasement early. After taking office, he went on a world-wide speaking tour, a good portion of it in the Middle East. The trip was billed as a diplomatic listening tour. But this "listening" tour turned into an apology trip.

In every speech, President Obama managed to say sorry for something America had done. The Heritage Foundation provides the most exhaustive listing of excerpts from those speeches[21]. Reading them is astonishing.

1. Apology to France and Europe ("America Has Shown Arrogance")

Speech by President Obama, Rhenus Sports Arena, Strasbourg, France, April 3, 2009.

"So we must be honest with ourselves. In recent years we've allowed our Alliance to drift. I know that there have been honest disagreements over policy, but we also know that there's something more that has crept into our relationship. In America, there's a failure to appreciate Europe's leading role in the world. Instead of celebrating your dynamic union and seeking to partner with you to meet common challenges, there have been times where America has shown arrogance and been dismissive, even derisive."

2. Apology to the Muslim World ("We Have Not Been Perfect")

---

21 http://www.heritage.org/europe/report/barack-obamas-top-10-apologies-how-the-president-has-humiliated-superpower#_ftn8

President Obama, interview with *Al Arabiya*, January 27, 2009. [2]

> *"My job to the Muslim world is to communicate that the Americans are not your enemy. We sometimes make mistakes. We have not been perfect. But if you look at the track record, as you say, America was not born as a colonial power, and that the same respect and partnership that America had with the Muslim world as recently as twenty or thirty years ago, there's no reason why we can't restore that."*

3. Apology to the Summit of the Americas ("At Times We Sought to Dictate Our Terms")

President Obama, address to the Summit of the Americas opening ceremony, Hyatt Regency, Port of Spain, Trinidad and Tobago, April 17, 2009.[3]

> *"All of us must now renew the common stake that we have in one another. I know that promises of partnership have gone unfulfilled in the past, and that trust has to be earned over time. While the United States has done much to promote peace and prosperity in the hemisphere, we have at times been disengaged, and at times we sought to dictate our terms. But I pledge to you that we seek an equal partnership. There is no senior partner and junior partner in our relations; there is simply engagement based on mutual respect and common interests and shared values. So I'm here to launch a new chapter of engagement that will be sustained throughout my administration.*

Kiara Ashanti

The United States will be willing to acknowledge past errors where those errors have been made."

4. Apology at the G-20 Summit of World Leaders ("Some Restoration of America's Standing in the World")

News conference by President Obama, ExCel Center, London, United Kingdom, April 2, 2009.[4]

"I would like to think that with my election and the early decisions that we've made, that you're starting to see some restoration of America's standing in the world. And although, as you know, I always mistrust polls, international polls seem to indicate that you're seeing people more hopeful about America's leadership.

I just think in a world that is as complex as it is, that it is very important for us to be able to forge partnerships as opposed to simply dictating solutions. Just to try to crystallize the example, there's been a lot of comparison here about Bretton Woods. "Oh, well, last time you saw the entire international architecture being remade." Well, if there's just Roosevelt and Churchill sitting in a room with a brandy, that's an easier negotiation. But that's not the world we live in, and it shouldn't be the world that we live in."

5. Apology for the War on Terror ("We Went off Course")

President Obama, speech at the National Archives, Washington, D.C., May 21, 2009.[5]

"Unfortunately, faced with an uncertain threat, our government made a series of hasty decisions. I believe that many of these decisions were motivated by a sincere desire to protect the American people. But I also believe that all too often our government made decisions based on fear rather than foresight; that all too often our government trimmed facts and evidence to fit ideological predispositions. Instead of strategically applying our power and our principles, too often we set those principles aside as luxuries that we could no longer afford. And during this season of fear, too many of us—Democrats and Republicans, politicians, journalists, and citizens—fell silent.

In other words, we went off course. And this is not my assessment alone. It was an assessment that was shared by the American people who nominated candidates for President from both major parties who, despite our many differences, called for a new approach—one that rejected torture and one that recognized the imperative of closing the prison at Guantanamo Bay."

6. Apology for Guantanamo in France ("Sacrificing Your Values")

Speech by President Obama, Rhenus Sports Arena, Strasbourg, France, April 3, 2009.[6]

"Our two republics were founded in service of these ideals. In America, it is written into our founding documents as "life, liberty, and the pursuit of happiness." In France: "Liberté"—absolutely—"egalité, fraternité." Our moral authority is derived from the fact that generations of our

citizens have fought and bled to uphold these values in our nations and others. And that's why we can never sacrifice them for expedience's sake. That's why I've ordered the closing of the detention center in Guantanamo Bay. That's why I can stand here today and say without equivocation or exception that the United States of America does not and will not torture.

In dealing with terrorism, we can't lose sight of our values and who we are. That's why I closed Guantanamo. That's why I made very clear that we will not engage in certain interrogation practices. I don't believe that there is a contradiction between our security and our values. And when you start sacrificing your values, when you lose yourself, then over the long term that will make you less secure."

7. Apology before the Turkish Parliament ("Our Own Darker Periods in Our History")

Speech by President Obama to the Turkish Parliament, Ankara, Turkey, April 6, 2009.[7]

"Every challenge that we face is more easily met if we tend to our own democratic foundation. This work is never over. That's why, in the United States, we recently ordered the prison at Guantanamo Bay closed. That's why we prohibited—without exception or equivocation—the use of torture. All of us have to change. And sometimes change is hard.

Another issue that confronts all democracies as they move to the future is how we deal with the past. The United

States is still working through some of our own darker periods in our history. Facing the Washington Monument that I spoke of is a memorial of Abraham Lincoln, the man who freed those who were enslaved even after Washington led our Revolution. Our country still struggles with the legacies of slavery and segregation, the past treatment of Native Americans.

Human endeavor is by its nature imperfect. History is often tragic, but unresolved, it can be a heavy weight. Each country must work through its past. And reckoning with the past can help us seize a better future."

8. Apology for US Policy toward the Americas ("The United States Has Not Pursued and Sustained Engagement with Our Neighbors")

Opinion editorial by President Obama: "Choosing a Better Future in the Americas," April 16, 2009.[8]

"Too often, the United States has not pursued and sustained engagement with our neighbors. We have been too easily distracted by other priorities, and have failed to see that our own progress is tied directly to progress throughout the Americas. My Administration is committed to the promise of a new day. We will renew and sustain a broader partnership between the United States and the hemisphere on behalf of our common prosperity and our common security."

9. Apology for the Mistakes of the CIA ("Potentially We've Made Some Mistakes")

Kiara Ashanti

Remarks by the President to CIA employees, CIA Headquarters, Langley, Virginia, April 20, 2009.[9] The remarks followed the controversial decision to release Office of Legal Counsel memoranda detailing CIA-enhanced interrogation techniques used against terrorist suspects.

> *"So don't be discouraged by what's happened in the last few weeks. Don't be discouraged that we have to acknowledge potentially we've made some mistakes. That's how we learn. But the fact that we are willing to acknowledge them and then move forward, that is precisely why I am proud to be President of the United States, and that's why you should be proud to be members of the CIA."*

10. Apology for Guantanamo in Washington ("A Rallying Cry for Our Enemies")

President Obama, speech at the National Archives, Washington, D.C., May 21, 2009.[10]

> *"There is also no question that Guantanamo set back the moral authority that is America's strongest currency in the world. Instead of building a durable framework for the struggle against al Qaeda that drew upon our deeply held values and traditions, our government was defending positions that undermined the rule of law. In fact, part of the rationale for establishing Guantanamo in the first place was the misplaced notion that a prison there would be beyond the law—a proposition that the Supreme Court soundly rejected. Meanwhile, instead of serving as a tool to counter terrorism, Guantanamo became a symbol that*

helped al Qaeda recruit terrorists to its cause. Indeed, the existence of Guantanamo likely created more terrorists around the world than it ever detained.

So the record is clear: Rather than keeping us safer, the prison at Guantanamo has weakened American national security. It is a rallying cry for our enemies."

On the one hand, the remarks and tenor of all the speeches are in keeping with traditional Progressive Liberal thought. America is always the evil one. The world's ills are generated and created by America. The Left is happy to live here and use the Constitution to propagate their views, but when it comes to sticking up for America itself, they skip that train. President Obama is a classical liberal. He might not call America evil, but as these excerpts from his tour and other speeches made later in his term as President show, he believes that America is lacking morally. He does not believe in the idea of American Exceptionalism. America is not THE nation; it is just one of many nations to him.

If all we had to deal with were laissez-faire European countries on issues of trade, the notion would be fine. Annoying to hear from the leader of your own the country, but not dangerous. However, we live in a world with countries like Iran, North Korea, Russia, and terrorists who despise Western society. These countries take their cues on what to do, attempt, or engage in from the actions and words of American leaders—especially the President. When you have a string of speeches that showcase you apologizing for American "missteps and behavior" it is considered weak. The cultures of the Middle East and Russia respect strength, and its projection—meaning that even if you do not mean to attack, or cannot attack, you still act like you can.

Take Iraq as an example. Saddam Hussein knew he did not have the army to defeat the US in any battle. He knew he did not have the material for a nuclear bomb. He may have used up all his stockpiles of chemical weapons on the Kurds (yes, Iraq did have chemical weapons of mass destruction[22]), but he acted like he had more. The feint eventually caught up with him, but only because of 9/11. If the Twin Towers had not gone down, he likely would still be the leader of Iraq. The point is that he acted like he was strong the entire time. It is a cultural norm within the Muslim world. You make people do things, or act like you can. You do not make nice.

Obama tried to make nice over everything he perceived that America had done since the founding of the country. The reason for this is twofold. One, he believes every word he uttered in those speeches. Two, he wanted to lessen the tensions between the US and the world, especially as it pertained to the war on terror.

It is the same thinking behind Chamberlain's view on Hitler. Chamberlain did not want to fight a war. That emotional stance allowed Chamberlain to fool himself into believing that Hitler had some sort of legitimate beef over how War World One ended for Germany and the six million Germans who lived in Czechoslovakia. Except that Hitler was never interested in reconciliation or diplomacy. He had his own goals.

The Islamic Jihadist terrorists who wish to destroy Western society are not interested in making nice. We know this because they keep attacking people. Europe has bent over backward for them, and they still get attacked. Al Qaeda and ISIS routinely send suicide bombers to kill *other Muslims*. Why would Obama think

---

22 https://en.wikipedia.org/wiki/Halabja_chemical_attack

sitting down for a chat, and refusing to say the words "Islamic Jihadist terrorism" would somehow change their minds?

November 5, 2009.

Army Major Nidal Hassan fatally shoots 13 fellow veterans and wounds 30 others. According to survivors, Hassan bowed and then screamed "Allahu Akbar" before opening fire. The words mean Allah is Greater in Arabic. It is the modern war cry of terrorists. Investigative reporting on the situation following the days after the shooting proved the Army had known Hassan was becoming radicalized. All evidence showed without a shadow of a doubt that Islamist terrorism and jihadist thinking were the motivation. To this day, neither President Obama nor his officials will call the attack terrorism. The government classified the shooting as "workplace violence." Furthermore, the term terrorism was stricken from use in government communications. It was replaced with the term "man-caused disaster."

September 11, 2012.

Members of the Islamic militant group Ansar al-Sharia attack the American embassy in Benghazi, Libya. Ambassador Christopher Stevens is killed. It is the first death of a US Diplomat in 33 years. USFS officer Sean Smith, and CIA contractors Tyrone Woods and Glen Doherty also lose their lives. President Obama does not directly call the attack a terrorist attack. Instead, he uses a vague phrase, claiming that "acts of terror" will not be tolerated.

The motivation given for the attack was an internet video either attacking or disparaging Islam. As you sit reading this book, the director of the video in question, Nakoula Basseley, sits in jail. The narrative is a simple. The video was released; it was seen by devout Muslims who had gathered in a spontaneous demonstration, and then attacked the compound of the ambassador in misplaced retaliation.

When you consider that President Obama created his whole Presidency on the power of words, you would think he knows better than to call these anything other than "terrorist acts" on both accounts. An act of terror can be me cutting you off on the highway. It is not, however, terrorism. Terrorism is not just violence against someone else. It is violence against someone else motivated by political or religious zealotry.

The idea that Benghazi was caused by a video is beyond stupid. Yet, President Obama made the assertion on the Late Show with David Letterman, in a speech to the United Nations, and by far the worst, in front of the caskets of the fallen soldiers with Hillary Clinton by his side.[23][24][25] I fail to see how Americans allowed the President to get away with such a blatant lie. The attackers had large ordnance and guns. Eighteen hours before the attack, al-Qaeda leader Ayman al-Zawahiri released an actual video calling for attacks on 9/11 that same year for the death of Abu Yahya al-Libi three months earlier. The attack was coordinated in its execution. To this day, President Obama has not disavowed the accusation of a video as the reason for the attack.

These are but two examples of how President Obama would go out of his way to avoid calling out Islamic terrorists. He has said more than once that the term is one that is useful. It is his belief, and the belief of others, that rhetoric like that is a recruiting tool. It makes it sound like America is at war with Islam, and we are not.

---

23 https://www.youtube.com/watch?v=dpKuFucvbww
24 https://www.youtube.com/watch?v=oBb2EQmtnhQ
25 https://www.youtube.com/watch?v=QSooz2wXpes

The problem, however, is when someone else decides that they are at war with you, then you are at war. You can sit around and act like you do not want to fight them, but they are still going to attack you. America does not hate Islam, but the problem with Islamic jihadists is *they do* hate you because you are Christian.

OH WAIT! Are you not a Christian? Are you Jewish? That is cool; jihadists hate you more. Hold up! Are you not Jewish either? In fact, you do not believe in any religion or God, correct? Outstanding! Jihadists both hate and have no respect for you. You are an unbeliever of any sort, therefore off with your head.

President Obama's refusal to call terrorism by its rightful name, Islamic jihadist terrorism, is nothing more than a signal of a bigger problem. He believes that you can talk to anyone. That everyone on the planet is essentially the same and values the same things in life. That is a false belief. In 1940 the Nazis did not value the same things as normal people. In 2009 through 2016, and in 2017, Islamic jihadist terrorists do not value what normal people value. Anyone who does not accept that fact is starting from a losing position.

THE GREAT
BEAR AWAKENS

In the 2012 Presidential debate, Barack Obama used his classic, professorial tone of voice to mock Mitt Romney's statements about Russia. Governor Romney made the assertion that Russia was America's greatest geopolitical threat. President Obama's exact words were:

*"Gov. Romney, I'm glad you recognize al-Qaeda is
a threat, because a few months ago when you were asked,*

*"What is the biggest geopolitical group facing America?"
you said Russia—not al-Qaeda. And the 1980s are now
calling to ask for their foreign policy back—because the
Cold War has been over for 20 years. But Governor, when
it comes to our foreign policy, you seem to want to import the
foreign policies of the 1980s, just like the social policy of the
1950s, and the economic policies of the 1920s.*

It was a cute line, funny even if you weren't an Obama supporter. Do you know what was even funnier? That hot mic moment between President Obama and President Medvedev that went thusly, *"This is my last election. After my election, I have more flexibility."*

Flexibility for what?

At the time, soon-to-be-President-again Vladimir Putin had a problem with America placing a missile defense shield in Poland and Romania. The US policy was that the missiles would be there to protect Europe from possible attacks from rogue nations like Iran. Russia believed, rightly, that it could have been used against them if Moscow ever decided to get a little frisky on the continent. Putin also took a dim view of the possibility of the country of Ukraine becoming a part of NATO.

For all the talk about current President Trump being a wide-eyed nationalist, it is Putin who is a true nationalist. The breakup of the Soviet Union never sat well with Putin. This is well documented in Putin's economic thesis. The paper lays out a reasoned (in his mind) argument for why Russia is weaker in its current form, and how it can regain its power and territories. It is a road map—one he has been following to a New Russia. Putin wants Russia back on top, and he wants its former territories back under the Great Bears' shadow. That is not as easy today as back before the Cold

War. Today you have NATO and the United States as barriers to that goal.

NATO, of course, was formed after World War II. The treaty's purpose was to serve as a deterrent to any future country or dictator who tries to take over like Hitler did. Any attack on one member nation is an attack on all the members and a call to war with everyone. The member states would band together and fight the aggressive nation. That is the concept. It has not been tested since its inception in any concrete way. Putin saw an opportunity in the lack of resolving in the member nations of NATO and the US when it came to the War on Terror.

The threat from Islamic terrorists was obvious, but after years of war, the will to fight them was waning. By the time Obama took office in 2009; the multinational coalition was only that on paper. America was carrying most of the load and expense. The US at one point had 150,000 troops in Iraq. The next highest country was Britain, at 46,000. Australia, 2,000. All the rest of the countries had less than a thousand. Still, many were clamoring to withdraw.

Putin smelled weakness. He was betting that any moves he made in Europe, or demands he made at the United Nations, would not be fought vigorously. He tested this theory in 2008 with the invasion of South Ossetia and Abkhazia, provinces of Georgia.

It is important to point out that the invasion in 2008 was the culmination of years of machinations, tensions, and small incursions under the Bush years. Simply, the problem began under President Bush, who was preoccupied with Iraq.

Russia has always claimed that the two aforementioned provinces are independent, with largely a Russian population, so if they wish to "return" to Russia, it is their right. That was the underlying excuse for sending in troops.

Georgia is a member of NATO. Sending troops into their country, whatever the excuse, is by treaty an attack on the US. Putin bet that with Bush about to leave office, the US would not enter a conflict with Russia.

He was correct. President Bush made a lot of noise, condemned the action, but did nothing. He did not have the political capital to launch an attack on a nuclear power on his way out the door.

In comes Obama with talk of withdrawing from Iraq, shutting down Gitmo, and his apology tour. Putin knew he would not get staunch resistance. He did get a nice photo op with Secretary of State and Russian Foreign Minister with a red reset button.

I believe it is not—even if he signed on for the job—fair to expect President Obama to come into the office and clean up a mess like Georgia after the fact. It is one thing to take over the reins of a war like Iraq, and quite another thing to start a new one on another continent. However, the situation in Georgia was a clear signal that Russia needed to be watched.

This is where the parallel between Obama and Chamberlain becomes clearer. Putin had shown his hand. The move on Georgia was as clear as Hitler's move to annex Austria. Chamberlain's and other European leaders' response was the Munich Agreement, ceding Czechoslovakia to Germany. Obama's response to Russia was a reset button. A new diplomacy effort, free of the aggressive cowboy style of Bush, would permeate all foreign affairs.

The reset ultimately leads to a resetting of American policy. The missile defense shield program for Eastern Europe was scrapped. The Guardian reported the reasons for this decision like this[26]:

_____

26 https://www.theguardian.com/world/2009/sep/17/missile-defence-shield-barack-obama

Commander-in-Failure

"Obama announced the reversal officially at a news conference today. "This new approach will provide capabilities sooner, build on proven systems to offer greater defences to the threat of attack than the 2007 European missile defence programme," he said.

He phoned the leaders of Poland and the Czech Republic last night to tell them he had dropped plans to site missile interceptors and a radar station in their respective countries. Russia had furiously opposed the project, claiming it targeted Moscow's nuclear arsenal.

The change of tack had been prompted by advances in missile technology and new intelligence about Iran's existing missile capabilities, Obama said.

The US president said "updated intelligence" on Iran's existing short- and medium-range missiles showed they were "capable of reaching Europe". He added that the US would continue its efforts to end Iranian attempts to develop an "illicit nuclear programme".

He said: "To put it simply our new missile defence architecture in Europe will provide

STRONGER, SMARTER, SWIFTER DEFENCES OF
AMERICAN FORCES AND AMERICA'S ALLIES."

I chose this set of remarks for a reason. They demonstrate a total lack of coherent thought. The missile defense shield was to protect Europe from possible missiles from Iran. Obama gets rid of the program, and then says in his remarks that "US intelligence shows Iran has missiles that could reach Europe." If that is the case, then why in the hell is Obama getting rid of the program that is designed to guard against a possible attack from Iran?

The answer is because that's what Russia wanted. Obama decided to give up something in the hopes that it would lead to better relations. It was a hallmark of his philosophy. Show America is willing to not be the bully.

The program died in 2009. Obama pledged flexibility in 2011. In 2014 Russia annexed Crimea. The reason given by Russia is that the population of ethnic Russians wanted to be independent and rejoin Russia. Does this not sound familiar?

When the Russians moved into Crimea what did President Obama do?

He gave another one of his father-figure speeches, with lines like:

> "Once again, we are confronted with the belief among some that bigger nations can bully smaller ones to get their way. That recycled maxim that might, somehow, makes right. So, I come here today to insist that we must never take for granted the progress that has been won here in Europe and advanced around the world, because the contest

of ideas continues for your generation, and that's what's at
stake in Ukraine today."

Pretty words that lead to nothing.

When Iraq invaded Kuwait, President George H. Bush told them to get out. He told them to leave or else. Saddam stayed; Bush declared war and kicked Iraq out of Kuwait. Bold, decisive, and commanding.

Russia is not Iraq. We probably cannot bitch-slap them like we can Middle Eastern countries. Plus, few Americans want a war with Russia over the Ukraine. Putin knew that and took advantage. The calculation was simple. We were not willing to do anything with Georgia, a NATO ally, and certainly not over Ukraine, a non-NATO country.

But the war was not the only course of action. Russia did not just bum-rush Crimea. They put tanks on the borders. They feinted first to see what we would do, what Obama would do. Obama could have simply given Ukraine US weapons. He could have sent some tanks to hang out on the other side of the border. He could have done something other than yapping his mouth about getting along. That is what projecting strength looks like. You can talk all you want about cooperation and the need for countries to respect each other, but damned well demonstrate there is a possible cost if respect is not given. You say, "I am not going to cross this line and hit you. But if you cross this line and hit me, then I will retaliate."

Some people would say that is an attitude only appropriate for attacks on America. Crimea is not America. Crimea and Ukraine are not in NATO. We have no national interests there. That is a shallow and short-sighted way to look at the problem. Sometimes, you punch the bully to protect someone you don't know because you know the bully also wants to hit you or your friends.

In the run-up to World War II, Austria, Czechoslovakia, France, Poland, etc., were not America. Hitler was demonstrating; however, that he would be a problem for everyone soon. Ukraine is not America. Georgia is not America. Neither are Estonia, Latvia, and Lithuania. All of the latter three are part of NATO. Putin wants all three back. You put tanks in Crimea and give Ukraine US weapons, just to show Putin his dreams of a New Soviet Union are just that—dreams.

Once Chamberlain championed and then signed the Munich Agreement, Hitler knew his dream of the Third Reich was possible. Obama turned down Ukraine's plea for military aid. Behind the scenes, they made it clear that Ukraine would have to eat the loss of the region and accept the Accession Treaty. Russia has been sanctioned by the UN, but they got what they wanted. Putin also got confirmation, like Hitler, that his dream of a New Soviet Union is possible, both in terms of land in Europe and influence in the world.

THE LINE THAT DIDN'T EXIST

George H. Bush was quite clear on what Saddam Hussein should do when Iraq invaded Kuwait. Bush gave him about five months and then carried through with his threat. War erupted, and coalition forces led by the US kicked Iraq out.

During Bill Clinton's term, ethnic cleansing began in Kosovo. The US State Dept. estimates 10,000 Albanians were killed, and 800,000 fled the Yugoslav forces. No doubt human rights were being violated in ways not seen in decades within Europe. Nonetheless, the UN Security council would not sign off on retaliation. President Clinton, along with Prime Minister Tony Blair, ignored the UN and got NATO to begin strikes. The President of Yugoslav, Slobodan Milošević, was warned. He was given a chance to stop the killings and control his troops. He did not. He paid the price.

To this day there is still confusion about what lead to the Iraq War. If you pull aside the conspiracy theory rhetoric from the Left and the Right, it will really come down to one thing. Saddam kept acting like he had weapons of mass destruction. We now know that the US *and several other countries including Israel, Russia, France, England, and Jordan* had bad intel about WMD's. What few people remember is that war could have been averted if Saddam had just let the weapons inspectors, mandated by the agreements signed after the Gulf War, into the country. Saddam refused, thinking the US would not attack. Bush carried through on his promise.

You can have any opinion on the Iraq War, or war in general. What is not up for debate is that no leader, especially a US President, can make a threat and not carry through on it. It is the definition of weakness and poor leadership. Weak because you should do what you tell the world you will do. Poor leadership because if you are not inclined to do something, you have no business making a threat.

There is no mistake, bad decision, or poor choice of words that will haunt Obama's legacy more than the "Red Line" comment thrown at Syrian President Bashar Assad. The US, smartly, did not wish to get into another engagement in a middle eastern country. Yet, the continued reports of human rights abuses were gaining coverage and countries were looking at what to do. Then reports, unconfirmed at first, began to come in that President Assad was using chemical weapons against rebel forces and civilians. The news eventually led to this statement from President Obama:

Kiara Ashanti

"We have been very clear to the Assad regime, but also to other players on the ground, that a red line for us is we start seeing a whole bunch of chemical weapons moving around or being utilized. That would change my calculus. That would change my equation."

It is one of the most famous lines of Obama's Presidency, because Assad did use chemical weapons, and Obama did nothing. He made the threat and then did not follow through.

When he made the remark, he was criticized for saying it. Why make it public in such a bold way, if you do not plan to follow through? It is possible that is was just another political line designed to make the President look tough and outraged over the use of internationally banned weapons. If so, his speech writer should be jailed, and the key thrown away for dereliction of duty. Even a political neophyte knows you cannot put a line like that in a speech for sake of appearances when it implies military action if the President's words are not heeded.

"The president was looking for a way to not have to make good on the threat that he had made," Col. Andrew Bacevich (Ret.), author of *The Limits of Power*, recounts Bacevich in an interview with PBS Frontline. *"I think because the President, having drawn that red line, realized that he had no appetite for direct military engagement in Syria."*

It would be easy to say; you cannot go to war just because you said you would. A deeper calculus when it comes to human lives and the lives of our troops must be taken. That is a valid point, which begs the question: Why say it? Why puff your chest out, if you know you are not going to do anything?

Only Obama knows the answer to that question. The problem, however, is these things do not happen in a vacuum. The whole world is watching. Russia, North Korea, China, ISIS, and other bad actors are watching what you are doing and saying. Once you say, "Do not do this, or else" and the *or else* never comes, your enemies know they can push you.

Obama escaped further pressure and ridicule thanks to the Russians. Russia struck a deal with Assad. Hand their chemical weapons over to them, and Syria and Obama could both avoid military action from the US. President Obama seemed pleased with the outcome, and to this day will either say he never gave a 'red line' or that he believed backing down was a better outcome.

I say Obama was pleased with the outcome, but that is a huge understatement. As is usually his practice, when Obama determined that he knew better than us poor rubes, he took to the stage to give us a message. In a speech given at MacDill Air Force base on December 6th, 2016, President Obama said the following:

> *"Just think about what we have been able to accomplish in the last eight years without firing a shot. We eliminated Syria's declared chemical weapons program. All of these steps have helped keep us safe and our troops safe. Those are the results of diplomacy…"*

Of course in week ten of America's new President, Donald Trump, the world discovered that Syria had not gotten rid of all of its chemical weapons. President Assad used them against is own people—again. President Trump decided to send a warning, and sent fifty Tomahawk missiles into the base the chemical attacks were launched from. But why did President Obama even believe the words in his speech?

The answer is because he wanted to believe in the words in the agreement. It is easier to think we have solved a problem because we have a "signed agreement" than the alternative. Obama did not want to attack Syria in any capacity. Which is fine if that's your foreign policy philosophy, but you cannot also threaten to attack out loud and not follow through. No matter what. It shows weakness. Obama not only deferred to the Russians, but also did not get the outcome as we now know.

That is because Obama is always playing checkers and not chess.

In one fell swoop, Russia showed the world they are the nation of influence. If the US bullies you or asks something of you, ignore them and come to Russia. Putin has more influence in Syria and the Middle East than Russia has had since before the end of the Cold War. Russian planes are the ones free to fly sorties across Syria, not the US. Syria could be given economic sanctions by the US, but Russia is in a position to be Assad's economic bulwark.

In August 2016, Wall Street reporter Jay Solomon told MSNBC[27] that the real reason the Obama administration backed off the "red line" was because Obama wanted a nuclear deal with Iran. Solomon reports that the comment was made when US negotiators were meeting secretly in Oman with Iran. Iran said if the US attacked Syria, they would walk away from the talks[28].

IRAN

There is a concept in contract negotiations that says, "Never want a deal so much that you are not willing to walk away from it." The idea is simple. If you cannot walk away from a deal, then you are willing to accept anything in order make a deal. You place

27 http://www.msnbc.com/andrea-mitchell-reports/watch/inside-the-us-iran-struggle-748574275947
28 http://www.businessinsider.com/obama-red-line-syria-iran-2016-8

yourself in a position of weakness because the other party knows that they can push and push and push. You will eventually accept terms that are bad for you.

Neville Chamberlain wanted to avoid fighting Hitler so much, he was willing to ignore what Hitler had already done, and hand over another country in the name of "peace in our time." Peace never came until Churchill fought.

President Obama decided at some point that he needed a foreign policy legacy. He wanted a grand flourish with which could he leave office. It could not be anything regarding Israel and the Palestinians. The well between him and Prime Minister Benjamin Netanyahu was too poisoned, mainly because Obama generally sided with the Palestinians.

For whatever reason, he decided on Iran. For decades, US Presidents have been telling Iran to stop trying to get nuclear weapons. We have sanctioned them, boxed them in, and subtly threatened war if they get close. Iran has ignored America and continued their nuclear objective, bit by slow bit.

President Obama determined that he would get Iran to stop their nuclear objective with the power of a negotiated deal. With words alone, he would do what no one else in the world could.

There is an undercurrent of mockery in my tone because the arrogance of the man is overwhelming. The US had sanctioned and seized billions of Iran dollars, forcing their economy into one that is barely functioning. The financial pain never stopped them. Beyond the corridor, deals and offers have been made over the years, to no avail. Smaller agreements have been made and broken. That is the history of Iran, but President Obama went full bore into negotiations with Iran.

141

The Iran nuclear deal has been derided by Republicans, while Democrats have run around saying that Obama had just stopped Iran's nuclear march. Here are the six things about it that matter.

1.   Each country interprets it differently.

In an effort to gain support, the Obama White House released a fact sheet on the deal. Iran immediately disputed the terms in the fact sheet. Either there was a misunderstanding on the words, or Iran was signaling, *as soon as we get our money, we are doing our own thing.*

2.   There are no enforcement measures.

The whole point of agreement from the US side is for Iran to take certain steps on dismantling their nuclear bomb program. If Iran fails to comply with the terms, then the consequence is… not stated. The deal only says a "dispute-resolution mechanism" will take effect. What that is is not stated.

3.   The final deal does not prevent a nuclear bomb.

The deal, if followed to a tee, only *delays* a bomb. It does not prevent it, something President Obama has admitted, although his surrogates claim it prevents a bomb. WTF?? What is even the point then?

4.   Iran gets the benefit of lifted sanctions without complying.

The Iran deal is front loaded for them. The sanctions were lifted immediately, moving 100 billion dollars back into Iran's coffers. In addition, their oil can now hit the worldwide market, with countries like Russia best positioned to get it. But since the deal is front-loaded, they don't have to demonstrate anything. Obama gave them the carrot, and per point two, there is no stick.

5. The balance of power in the Middle East shifts.

Iran wants to dominate the Middle East. They have not had the power to do so. Now they will have the economic means to pursue that goal. Saudi Arabia, which dominates now, will fight to prevent Iran from rising—especially if Iran gets nukes. Saudi will want their own nukes. More importantly, if Iran looks like they are getting close, Israel will attack. The Muslims countries will put aside their dislike of each other, in solidarity of their hatred of the Jewish state.

6. The deal does not deal with human rights.

The Iran deal not only leaves out anything regarding human rights, it was likely never on the table. Iran is a religious theocracy. Officially it does not list itself as a Sharia law country, but multiple aspects of Sharia are engrained in their political and legal system. Rights for Christians or women were always going to be resisted.

What did America get out of this deal? The same thing my ex-fiancée got me for Valentine's Day, not a damned thing. Does the deal stop Iran's march toward a nuclear bomb? No, it only delays it. Does giving them $100 million and an open economy slow the march down any more than when we had their economy in a choke hold? The answer is obvious. What about economics? Is there some mineral or glaring economic interest we now have access to that we did not before? Umm, negative.

I struggle to see what the upside for America and the world is here? Seriously, if you put Democratic and Republican politics aside, what did we get that can be pointed to with clear-cut accuracy? How are we better today than three years ago?

In listening to all the interviews of Obama surrogates, supporters, and the President himself, the consensus seems to be that we now have a shot at Iran changing their behavior. We have given them a positive incentive to join the world stage. In other words, we have Hope that Iran will Change.

Chamberlain had Hope and a signed piece of paper that Hitler would not continue his war path. He believed in the words on the paper—and the words of Hitler himself—that war would cease. Obama had a signed piece of paper that he can point to and say, "I did that." When the paper gets ignored, he could, I guess, blame someone else.

President Obama made the same mistakes that Chamberlain made, repeatedly. He wanted to avoid conflict at nearly all costs. He ignored the actions and evidence in front of him and decided that because he wanted to be a different kind of leader, he could make things happen just because of it. He appeased Russia, Iran, and the Muslim world because he did not want conflict. In return, the seeds for worse conflict were being sown and watered.

Yes, President Obama did order the operation that killed Bin Laden. Yes, he increased troop levels in Afghanistan—though not at the levels needed or requested. He mastered the use of ordering a drone strike. Those are actions that cannot be denied, and can be called up to try and refute what I have laid out here. But understand this—those were all half measures, actions along the edges that did not and would not have any impact on the core issues.

He could have stopped Russia annexing Crimea. Russia is not quite ready for a true war with America, nor does it want one. A battalion of tanks in Crimea would have sent the Russians back to Moscow. It sends the message: "No, Vladimir the Great Bear is not coming back during my watch."

Immediate air strikes on Syria after the chemical weapon use tells Assad, Russia, and others: *Attack civilians in certain ways, and you will be punished, we mean what we say. International law will be enforced.*

Iran was a fool's dream. More people than Obama have proven to Iran that our threats were empty. If Bush would not attack, then certainly Obama was not going to do it. Iran secretly wanted and needed a deal to lift sanctions. They never showed their hand, though; Obama had already done so.

WATCHING MY BROTHER WORK

When it comes to foreign policy, racial politics usually take a backseat. By that, I mean whereas the black community will look at the actions of a President and evaluate them based on what is happening in the black community, that does not happen in foreign policy. The black community does not say, "we wish President Obama would do 'X' because he's black," regarding foreign affairs.

Leaving racial politics out is a good thing. It would be nice if it could happen in other areas. The absence of racial politics, however, shifts the focus from what the President is doing for me and mine to a conversation about his leadership qualities. When it comes to President Obama, watching that shift in fellow blacks is an interesting event.

Presidents are usually evaluated on two general principles regarding foreign policy: whether they are strong or weak. The nuances of leadership styles such as collaborative, steadfast, decisive, etc. get lost in most conversations. Strong or weak is the general standard. It is a bit shallow, but it does make for easy sound bites on television and in news studies.

The black community—or rather, the individuals who claim to speak for the community—did not view Obama in either vein. African-Americans seemed to prefer descriptions like cool, or hip. MSNBC commentator Touré is famous for saying, "Obama is just so cool. He's a cool cat."

I would write posts on Facebook about his foreign policy decisions, and inevitably in the comments, at least two people (sometimes more) would talk about how cool is Obama. Calm, cool, and collected.

I found this irritating.

America does not need a President who is hip, cool, or someone who looks like they would be fun to hang out with at the club. We need decisive leaders who understand the stakes. As a black man looking at the brother in the White House fail time and again, or demonstrate indecisiveness, I felt embarrassed at times.

That statement is ironic to many a black democrat. As far as most black people are concerned, individuals like myself, Alan West, Ben Carson, Michael Steele, or Herman Cain are embarrassments. How can we put down the black President? How can we criticize him in the same way that white people do?

Do we not know we are black?

For the record, myself, Herman Cain, Dr. Carson, and every other black conservative are aware we are black. We see ourselves in the mirror every morning. When we look at our reflection, we do not consciously OR unconsciously hate what we see. And not for nothing, but if we were to ever forget, plenty of liberal black democrats would have no problem pointing it out to us.

We have decided to follow the principle of Dr. Martin Luther King to its logical conclusion, "judge a man by the content of his character, not the color of his skin." Ergo, just because "brother Barack" is a black man, that does not mean he gets unwavering support by default. I certainly do not remember the black community embracing Clarence Thomas, Condi Rice, and Herman Cain. However, I do remember the black community turning on Dr. Carson the moment he became critical of President Obama.

It appears that color AND political affiliation matter more than character, results, or decision making.

I'm really happy that it makes black people feel great to see President Obama singing, dancing on Ellen, or walking with swag (urban term for "swagger") when he gets off Air Force One. I wonder, though, where was that swag when he walked to the negotiating table with Iran? Why was he so damned meek with Putin?

Why is *Mr. Cool Cat with swag*'s second most famous foreign policy line "Lead from Behind?" Leading from behind???? What nonsense is that?

In the immortal words of Ricky Bobby, "If you're aren't winning, you're losing."

This Harvard-educated man came into office with a brilliant mind (supposedly) and somehow managed to not elevate our stature in the world, but lower it. Many foreign leaders like Obama, but do not respect him. Foreign leaders who are adversaries to America believe he is weak, which means they see America as weak.

Obama supporters would say that is not true, or is unfair. The proof is in this question. If you are Estonia, Latvia, or Lithuania, and Russia is prowling your border, do feel as if you can count on America?

This was so frustrating to watch. I wanted this guy to do well. I did not want him to fail. I wanted him to figure it out as Bill Clinton had done. And yes, I wanted America to see what the black guy could do. I hoped against hope that I would be wrong in my initial assessment of Obama before he won the election.

I can tell you for certain, I did not enjoy the attacks from my community. As I have pointed out more than once, rejecting Democrats is one thing; rejecting the first black President is anathema. It's like going back in time two thousand years to when people lived amongst tribes and rejected the chosen tribal leader. Luckily, I live in a time where I do not have to be worried about getting kicked out of the village and eaten by lions.

Do not believe, however that there was no cost. I had spoken to my high school sweetheart on a regular basis for years—until Obama was elected and I rejected him. I have "friends" who believe I should get counseling because I "hate myself as a black man." I have fewer friends today than in 2007. Some of the friends who remain regularly make comments about my "weird beliefs" as if not wanting to see the unborn killed is the same as believing in alien abduction.

For all my wailing against the black community's expectations that I support Obama because he was black, it did hurt to not be able to do it. Every time I had to get into a debate or write an article critical of him, my stomach twisted. As I stated in the introduction, black Americans are hard-wired to want the person who looks like us to do well. A black conservative is not immune to that emotional pull; we are just not blinded by it.

I sat back and watched my brother, President Obama, work his foreign policy and wonder where his vaunted intellect went. Yes, he was black. Yes, he was expertly educated. Yes, it is obvious he has a high IQ. It was also obvious, however, that he would miss stuff the last four Presidents before him would not miss. He made decisions that not only proved to be bad decisions, but could be seen as bad even before the results appeared. I go back to the Chamberlain analogy. The only people who did not know how that agreement with Hitler would turn out are the people who signed the deal and their supporters. All you had to do was look at the evidence.

Chamberlain saw what he wanted, for either personal or political reasons. It cost him. It cost numerous countries. It almost cost England.

America is now faced with the same situation. Obama, either because of his personal temperament (some people are just not comfortable with conflict) or his political ideology, saw what he wanted. When reality slapped him in the face, he ignored it.

ISIS was spreading, but he called them the JV squad. He allowed Mubarak to be kicked out of Egypt, and we ended up with the Muslim Brotherhood. He made nice with Putin, and a piece of another country was taken over. He marked a redline, and it was crossed indiscriminately. Obama campaigned for re-election, saying al Qaeda was on the run, and then BAM, Benghazi happened.

In each instance, there were clear signs of what was really happening. Obama ignored them all, choosing instead to believe his own narrative. When that narrative proved to be incorrect, he then made the most egregious of sins. He denied the results.

Kiara Ashanti

Even Chamberlain had the good sense to admit he was wrong about Hitler. Obama admits nothing, and that is why he was a failure.

EPILOGUE: MORBID DÉJÀ VU

November 8, 2016

Wisconsin has just been called. The blue wall is broken. For the second time, an outsider has defeated the Clinton machine. Donald Trump is going to be the next President of the United States.

It is beyond improbable. He broke every political rule that has ever existed. The media portrayed him as having every *-ism* known to mankind. He never led in the polls. IT-WAS-JUST-NOT-POSSIBLE!

It was, however, going to be a reality. The race was not yet called; however, the writing was on the wall. Donald Trump was going to win. He would be President.

A surge of happy relief flooded my body, and then stopped cold. A blanket of déjà vu folded over me. There it was again… morbid fascination. I had felt it eight years ago; I felt it rising in me now. Except this time, I was in the group smiling at the oncoming light on the tracks.

Another potential train wreck was heading toward America, but for different reasons than Obama.

Obama had no executive experience. Trump had turned a million-dollar loan into a 10-billion-dollar company and world-wide brand. He was a CEO in an age where those without try to downplay business success as just dumb luck. He knew how to run something.

Trump also had zero political experience. He had never written laws or bills. He did not know how the inner workings of government operated. Worse, as a CEO he is used to telling someone to do something and it getting done. The government does not work in that manner. In politics, no one does what you say, just because you want it. Forces will gather against you under normal circumstances.

Trump winning the election was not normal. Only one major news outlet had people on it who were ecstatic, or calm. All the rest were crying, gnashing their teeth, and dumbfounded to the point of calling everyone who voted for Trump stupid racists.

Of course, they had called his supporters that before, but now the venom behind the words was acerbic. The line of the night went to CNN's Vann Jones, who called the election results a "white lash."

My initial euphoria had little to do with Trump. I was just glad that Hillary Clinton had lost. I also found the prospect of rubbing Trump's win in the face of sanctimonious Trump-haters glorious. My attitude had more to do with Liberals than any fondness for Donald Trump.

I had no doubt that he could be better than Clinton, but my attitude was tempered. For months, I had seen the same blind belief on the Republican side as I had when it came to Obama in 2008. It started with Ted Cruz, who said all the right things to conservatives but had no executive experience. Trump was saying some of the right things, but his take-no-prisoners, non-PC style is what people liked. After eight years of Obama and PC-nation as a policy, it invigorated people to hear someone say the same things they said on Facebook, in bars, and at the dinner table. Trump saying these things in the wrong ways was not relevant.

Trump voters were as giddy as the Obama voters in 2008 and 2012. The sense of optimism was also as high. Change was a-coming as far as Trump voters were concerned, and it could not come fast enough. Not for them anyway.

The streets of America did not clamor in open joy as in 2008. Trump supporters did the same thing they had during the campaign, sat back silently and smiled. The only sound was the wailing of horror and disbelief from Democrats that someone like *Donald Trump* had won. The wailing has not stopped since the election. Protests, violence, and anger fueled by fear have been in the headlines.

On some level, I understand—at least intellectually—the reaction. Liberals dislike Republicans, but they loathe Trump. In their eyes, the end of the Republic is nigh.

Here is the thing; I'm going to let you in on a little secret. Whatever you think of Donald Trump: racist, misogynist, sexist, ill-informed, rude, take your pick or add them all together, it does not matter. Donald Trump *ONLY* exists because of Barack Obama.

Everything liberals, Democrats, and the media despise about Trump, be they true or not, is now in the White House because of President Obama. He is the progenitor of Trump's win. Obama sowed the seeds for a Trump electoral win.

Under President Obama, the country went ten trillion dollars more into debt, in just eight years[29]. President Obama pushed an economic agenda that produced less than 2 percent annual growth.

29 http://www.businessinsider.com/national-debt-deficit-added-under-president-barack-obama-2017-1

Under President Obama, ninety million people stopped looking for work and remained on the sidelines.

President Obama told America they could keep their doctors, and then people lost them. He increased taxes and created new regulations; regulations that kept businesses hoarding cash, instead of expanding.

America's stature in the world has not increased, but decreased. ISIS is no longer just the name of an Egyptian goddess and 1970s Saturday morning television program. They are a cancer that metastasized under his watch.

America elected a black man with overwhelming numbers and support. But race relations are worse than they have been in decades. Political correctness is no longer just the polite way to say something at a dinner party, but an anchor of national and international policy.

These are the things President Obama has done. This is his true Presidential legacy. America is simply not better off than when he took office. The so-called great recession notwithstanding, two-percent growth is what you can get even if you do nothing. Obama did a lot; it was just all wrong.

If President Obama had managed to get three to four percent GDP growth, fifty million more people would have jobs today. If he had fixed healthcare just for the people who did not have it, rather than changing the whole system, rates would be lower than they are now. More importantly, the Tea Party would probably have never risen to the extent and success it did. If he had taken ISIS seriously, they would be around, but not as the critical problem they are now. Simply, if Obama had succeeded in the areas former Presidents had succeeded, it is likely Trump would never have happened.

154

Commander-in-Failure

Trump ran on doing the opposite of what America had seen for the last eight years. Hillary Clinton ran on continuing what America saw for the last eight years. Yet, liberals stand shocked that they lost?

What are they shocked over? Who wants two percent growth? Who wants to increase the debt their grandkids must pay? Why would millions of Americans like to be told what health care plan they must buy, and spend more money to do it? Does being called a racist for asking foreigners to fill out a green card form instead of coming through an underground tunnel sound like your idea of a fun time?

ISIS is cutting off heads. Lone-wolf terrorists are ramming groups of people with trucks in Europe and America. Roadside bombs are going off in Boston. Gay club goers are being stalked, and then shot while dancing. This is what has happened, and each time, the attackers scream "Allahu Akbar." Does your President make you feel safer by not calling it Islamic terrorism? Do you feel like he has a handle on it when news media reports the JV squad has taken over more territory?

No. No. And no.

As God is my witness, I am telling you Barack Obama's enduring legacy will not be the failures I have detailed here in this book. It will not be Obamacare. It will not, perhaps, even be having been voted in as the first black President. It will be the election of Donald Trump.

His failures as Commander-in-Chief opened the door for Trump. Supporters can scream to the high heavens about Obama being successful, but the proof of whether that is true or not is the blond guy sitting in the Oval Office.

If Obama had been the President the country needed, if he had been successful in the way his supporters and the black community claim him to be, then Trump would not be President. We might have Rubio, Kasich, or even Christie. We would not have President Trump.

We also would have a hell of a lot more Democrats in power across this land.

In 2009 the Democrats held the White House, Senate, and House of Representative with supermajorities. Democrat governors were all over the country. State legislators were evenly split between Republicans and Democrats.

Following behind President Obama and the tenor of his policies, as well as his political direction, Democrats have lost all of that ground. Republicans own the House. Republicans have retaken the Senate. They have taken the Oval Office. Nearly a thousand state legislature seats have been lost to Republicans. Thirty-three out of fifty governors' seats are Republican.

To put this into perspective, Republicans are literally one state away from being able to call a Constitutional Convention. They are a hairsbreadth away from being able to amend the Constitution.

This is what has occurred under Barack Obama. If you are a Democrat and hate Republicans, well your guy Obama has been the biggest boon for Republican success. If you are a Republican, then your party owes its success in the last eight years to Obama. Give him a high five, or a fist bump.

President Obama has been the leader of the Democrat party for the last eight years. They have been decimated under his leadership. Republicans say that America is not better off after Obama. The Democrat party could say the same thing.

Commander-in-Failure

Barack Obama failed to create a growing economy. He failed to make health care more affordable or work better. His Presidency did not lead to better race relations. Internationally, he projected weakness, not strength. He failed to celebrate the changes in America to the African-American community. He failed to name the problem and enemy in modern-day terrorism. Lastly, his brand of democratic liberalism failed to assist his party in elections across America.

And that is why Barack Obama is the Commander-in-Failure.

THANK YOU

Thank you for reading Commander-in-Failure. I hope that you learned something or at least discovered a different perspective. I also hope that you could get a sense that my critique on America's first black president is not based in hatred for the man personally. I pride myself on keeping things intellectually honest always.

If you enjoyed Commander, then the second-best thing you can do to help me, besides reading the book, is leave a review on the book at Amazon or Barnes and Noble. It will only take a minute or two to leave one, less if you are reading this on your tablet. I love honest feedback.

Be sure to go to my website and subscribe for updates on future political commentary. I'm a news junkie that likes to examine everything. I have some excellent issues I plan to get into the nitty-gritty about. I'd love to have you check those out too.

Thanks again.

Kiara Ashanti

@dredlockedrepub

http://kiaraashanti.com/home-splash/

Coming Soon

NATURAL BORN CONSERVATIVE

I get the question all the time from all types of people. A look of disbelief and shock usually accompanies the query.

"You're a *Republican?* How can that be?"

The "be" part of the question is usually at a higher vocal octave, emphasizing the state of disbelief in the questioner. I have gotten the reaction for years, decades even, and it still amuses me. In fairness, I cannot blame the incredulity.

I'm a black man. My name, Kiara Ashanti, is an African name. And by the way, I sport long dreadlocks as my hairstyle of choice. Whatever image a person may have in their head about how a black republican would look, I do not fit the image.

But Republican I am. Republican I have been, or leaned, as long as I can remember. I have no shame in the designation. I wear the mantle proudly and often loudly. I have never been in the political closet so to speak.

I have—or had—always chalked up the surprise at my political affiliation as the natural consequence of both whites and blacks not knowing any black republicans. One person once told me that it was easier to find a gay person than a black Republican. Even though I knew that based on pure numbers, that was false, I still could not argue against the sentiment. Blacks are known for many things: being great at sports, singing, dancing, and being Democrats. Before cable news and social media, the only black Republicans anyone might hear from or about in the public arena were Clarence Thomas, former Congressman Jesse Watts, and Colin Powell.

I thought Facebook and Twitter had definitively changed that. I routinely saw posts from other blacks like myself. People who had rejected the cultural hegemony in black America to be a dyed-in-the-wool Democrat. A post I made in 2012 changed all of that.

On April 28th, I did what millions of people worldwide do every day; I was checking my Facebook page. While reading the news feed of comments submitted by my Facebook connections, I noticed a striking picture in the instant news feed to the right. It was a picture of a black man, staring resolutely from the screen with the title, "You don't understand why I'm conservative." To the right of the black male were seven statements about why he was conservative. The words struck me instantly, because they were true, were on point, and summed up why I was conservative.

I decided to share the picture, but instead of just sharing it on my page, I went one step further. I saved the picture and uploaded it as my new timeline banner. I wanted the statement to be there for all to see when they came to my page.

I do that a lot in life. If something is worth saying, I say it loud, often, and strongly. If something is worth fighting for, then I fight hard. At the time, I did not think much of the post, beyond the idea that my democratic friends were going to be shaking their heads at me. After posting the picture, I went to bed.

The next morning when I did a quick Facebook check, I had sixty-five new friend requests and ten private messages. All of them were in response to the picture. I accepted all the requests and went on with my day. Later that afternoon, and I had fifty-two more friend requests and twelve more private messages. I accepted all those as well. Later that evening I signed in again, and again I had more friend requests—this time seventy-two. By the end of the weekend, I accepted four hundred new friends to my Facebook account. By the end of the month, I had 1,245 new friends. The picture in question has been shared over 1,545 times and counting on Facebook. One of my new friends edited the picture, putting my photo in place of the other one. That photo has been shared over 10,000 times and has to date 25,000 comments on the thread.

I do not know why the picture went on a mini-viral roll. I did not create the picture; I just shouted it to the mountain tops, so to speak, on my page. I can only imagine how many shares it got from the original poster. I do know this, though—the messages resonated in a deep fashion with conservatives. It touched them on an emotional level, on a visceral level. More important, every message I got was either one of admiration or questions about how other blacks react to my conservatism. Most felt the need for more information from me.

Why was I conservative? How could I be conservative? How could *any black person* be conservative?

This book is the answer; at least in part. Every black Republican has their own story or reasons for turning away from the Democratic party. Nonetheless, we have commonalities in our experience and reasoning. The huge response to this photo, and the questions that followed in its mini viral wake, tells me that people are desperate to understand.

Natural Born Conservative is my story about why I chose the Grand Ole Party and will provide insights into why public figures like Herman Cain, Condi Rice, Dr. Ben Carson, and others chose

Conservatism as well. It will expand on the seven tenets expounded in the photo that serves as the catalyst for me writing this book. In the end, you will know the path that leads me to conservatism, and you will know why millions of blacks and whites together have joined our path as well.

Made in the USA
Las Vegas, NV
02 January 2021